Three Minutes a Day

VOLUME 36

Other Christopher Books in Print

Better to Light One Candle
and other volumes in the
Three Minutes A Day
series

Day by Day with Jesus

God Delights in You

World Religions

THREE MINUTES A DAY
VOLUME 36

The Christophers

Msgr. Jim Lisante
Director

Stephanie Raha
Editor-in-Chief

Margaret O'Connell
Senior Research Editor

Joan Bromfield
Edward J. Devane
Jonathan Englert
Umberto Mignardi
Jerry O'Neil
Karen Hazel-Radenbaugh
Anna Marie Tripodi
Anne-Marie Welsh
Monica Ann Yehle-Glick
Contributing Editors

The Christophers
12 East 48th Street
New York, NY 10017

As God's chosen ones, holy and beloved,

clothe yourselves with compassion, kindness,

humility, meekness, and patience.

Bear with one another and,

if anyone has a complaint against another,

forgive each other;

just as the Lord has forgiven you,

so you also must forgive.

Above all, clothe yourselves with love,

which binds everything together

in perfect harmony.

COLOSSIANS 3:12-14

Introduction

In an age and society that expects us to cram our days with work and other activities, it's crucial to take at least a short time out for prayer and reflection. *Three Minutes a Day* can provide that break and, we hope, encourage you to use all the minutes of your life wisely. You might start by contemplating God's gift of time:

Lord, You give me today
one minute at a time.
That's all I have,
all I ever will have.

Give me the faith
that believes each moment
asks me to trust You
even as You trust me.

Give me the hope
that holds within each minute
– despite pain or doubt or fear –
an anticipation of eternity with You.

Give me the love
that transforms each minute
of my life into a reflection
of Your forgiveness, mercy and goodness. Amen.

May God bless all the minutes and all the years of your life.

The Christophers

Effective Resolutions

Every New Year's Day, many people resolve to do and be any number of things over the weeks and months to come. Often, with the best of intentions, these never come to pass.

Begin this year with effective resolutions by keeping these ideas in mind:

- Be realistic and positive. Learn from your mistakes. Think small, one day at a time.
- Be generous with praise. Avoid sarcasm. Develop a sense of humor and be able to laugh at yourself.
- Be alert, awake and aware. "Now" is all we have. Practice the art of patience. Practice forgiveness. Let go of negativity.

There are so many ways to use time well: read a book; go for a walk; help at a homeless shelter; complete unfinished projects; play games with the family; watch old home movies; meditate; bike; get a pet. Make the most of the time God has given you.

Prosper the work of our hands! (Psalm 90:17)

I pledge to live life fully and with integrity, Generous Giver.

A Woman, a Whisk, and a Victory

Life holds many undiscovered joys. But a keen eye and a willing heart can perceive many of them.

Take, for instance, Michael Ruhlman. A chef and author, he can turn the simple act of a family preparing a meal together into an epic event, a moment to be forever savored.

Ruhlman recalls how he and his father cheered his mother from the sidelines when she took on the challenge of making béarnaise sauce. "Mom didn't just make béarnaise," he writes, "she competed against it. Armed with a whisk and butter, (she) came out fighting." Victorious at the end of the battle, Ruhlman says filet mignon and béarnaise "meant celebration, happiness and good times, all of us together."

Better yet, he says the smell of reduced vinegar and tarragon bring him the same feelings today. "Except," he notes, "now we are four – my wife, our children and me." Memories help us savor our todays as much as our yesterdays.

Celebrate your festivals. (Nahum 1:15)

Help me remember, Lord, the joys of my past, and share them with those in my present.

How Warm Alaska Can Be...

In Fairbanks, Alaska, where 30 degrees below zero is not an unlikely temperature, it can be difficult to cope with the elements. The old saying encourages us to make lemonade when life gives us lemons, but what does one do when life gives one six months of ice? Kathleen Carlo-Kendall and Anita Tabor know the answer to that. With other positive minded women, they formed the first all-female team to enter the International Ice Art Championships held there each year.

When Fairbanks is frozen solid, these women are out chipping, scraping and shaping works of art out of the abundant ice. Their efforts offer relief from being shut indoors, provide practice for the team, and transform Fairbanks into an outdoor sculpture museum of uplifting imagery for all the citizens.

Circumstances in our own lives can feel as extreme as a cold Alaskan winter. Remember that you can make art out of your barricades with God's help.

Rely on the Lord. (Isaiah 36:7)

Keep me positive, Lord. Guide my heart and mind to the most positive way of viewing things.

Memo to Those in Charge

As every parent knows, even with the best intentions, it is hard to be sure what's best for your children. Fred Manocherian was reminded of that when he came across an anonymous list of "don'ts" from children to parents. It included:

- Don't spoil me. I'm only testing you.
- Don't take too much notice of my small ailments.
- Don't suggest that you are perfect or infallible.
- Don't let me form bad habits. I have to rely on you to detect them in the early stages.
- Don't be upset when I say, "I hate you". It isn't you that I hate, but your power to thwart me.

As God knows better than any of us, sometimes you have to let those you are nurturing make their own mistakes. Let us love our charges as He loves us.

Pursue peace with everyone. (Hebrews 12:14)

When someone needs my strength, remind me to offer them Yours as well, Almighty Father.

Say "Pulitzer!"

When humor columnist Dave Barry won the Pulitzer Prize some years ago, his editors asked him to stop by the office, withholding the news until they could tell him in person.

He arrived at the Miami Herald with his then 8-year-old son, Rob, thinking it would be a brief stop before the family left town for the weekend. Realizing what was about to happen – and understanding it would mean interviews and receptions–he told Rob their trip would have to be postponed.

"His face just fell," Barry told World Traveler magazine. So he promised his son a gift, in this case, a Nintendo game.

Rob hugged his dad, smiling from ear to ear just as the Pulitzer announcement was made. Photos were snapped and when the newspaper came out, colleagues told Barry it was gratifying to see how thrilled Rob was about the award.

Things may not always be quite what they seem. Enjoy a moment of humor whenever you can, especially with youngsters.

Be content. (Sirach 29:23)

Lord, keep me focused on the joy in my own life.

Into Africa

Bridget Studer is a speech therapist who had been home schooling her three children. John Studer is a dentist who always thought he would take a sabbatical to teach in Europe.

But when they began exploring opportunities abroad, John Studer found that, "God opened doors and guided us." Suddenly the family was in Africa learning a new language and preparing to help Christian missionaries adjust to life there through the Tamale Institute of Cross-Cultural Studies. The goal: help Westerners understand new cultures so they can more fully respond to the needs of the people.

Bridget Studer says, "God calls people. We are just an ordinary family like everyone else out there."

She's correct. God calls ordinary people, single and married, of every age, race, nationality, ethnicity and denomination to be the salt of the earth and light to the world.

You are the salt of the earth...You are the light of the world. A city built on a hill.
(Matthew 5:13,14)

May we dare to follow You, Lord God, whether it is across the street or across the world.

Include 'Em, or Lose 'Em

How can a manager keep his or her best talent from quitting to join the competition? Based on advice from one senior executive, money isn't necessarily the answer. Instead, give employees a chance to make a difference and feel important within the organization, and you may win their loyalty.

Ask key employees about their wants and needs regarding work satisfaction, and then outline a plan to make feasible requests become a reality. "Find out what motivates people and try to supply it," says Rosemary Dow of Lucent Technologies. "It's a sign of good faith, and it helps make them feel valued."

It's interesting: sometimes the best way to make a difference in the world is to give someone else that very opportunity. Best of all, that chance can be discovered everywhere: at work, home, or in your community. The opportunities are boundless.

Encourage one another. (1 Thessalonians 4:18)

Lord Jesus, help me recognize the opportunities for service that are presented to me every day.

A Habit Worth Having?

Almost 2000 years ago, the Greek philosopher Plutarch commented that "character is simply habit long continued." He was right. While we might be born with certain tendencies, our day-to-day behavior has a tremendous effect on our whole being.

Nearly 1800 years later, another philosopher, William James, addressed the same subject. He said, "Could the young but realize how soon they will become mere walking bundles of habits, they would give more heed to their conduct. ...We are spinning our own fates, good or evil, and never to be undone."

Your "bundle of habits" is a large part of what makes you *you*. But what about the idea that the result cannot be undone? Every habit has its start in one moment and breaking it begins the same way. If you want to change something, try. It is possible.

Unless you change and become like children you will never enter the kingdom of heaven. (Matthew 18:3)

Spirit of God, it is so hard to give up bad habits, so hard to persist in good ones. But with You all things are possible.

No Time to Help?

If you've been wondering whether you have the time to help others when your day is already tightly packed, consider these ideas from Danny Seo's book *Heaven on Earth.*

- Throw rock salt or a de-icing mixture on your sidewalk to help prevent people from falling.
- Donate used CD's to a public library. Or sell them to a used-music store and give the proceeds to charity.
- Take old eyeglasses to the Lion's Club or to a Lenscrafters store where they'll be refitted for use by a needy person.
- Bring voter registration forms to work and make them available.
- Keep the phone number of the humane society or wildlife rehabilitation center handy in case you spot an injured animal.

Maybe you don't appreciate how helpful you already are. Big efforts count, but so do lots of little things.

In Joppa there was a disciple whose name was Tabitha. ...She was devoted to good works and acts of charity. (Acts 9:36)

Encourage us, Father, to make time for those who need us.

Harvesting Self-Esteem

The New Orleans Kids Café is one of three hundred nationally sponsored by America's Second Harvest food banks to help feed needy children. But this café, opened in 1999 under the direction of Craig Cuccia, operates like a real restaurant. The waiters and most of the diners are school-aged kids, and they might go hungry if they couldn't eat there.

Children who work for a small stipend prepare the tables and sit down to a meal served by adult volunteers before the doors open for other kids. Adults also eat with the children, showing good table manners and encouraging conversation.

Many of the youngsters face problems at home from illiteracy to drug addiction. Cuccia says the café has developed self-esteem in those whose "environment tends to make them think they can't succeed, but this is something that shows them that they can."

How can we afford to let even one child fail? Each is of infinite value and can know success if given a chance.

Give good gifts to your children. (Matthew 7:11)

Inspire me to serve gladly, Lord.

Fighting Against Abuse

Since becoming UNICEF's executive director in 1995, former New York state senator and City Council president Carol Bellamy has seen firsthand how little protection women have against abuse.

Appalled by what she's seen, Bellamy hopes to place her organization at the center of a global drive for women's rights. Members have pressed local officials to implement domestic-abuse legislation, held workshops for local judges and have asked police forces to hire more women. "You try to get your messages out in whatever way you can," says Bellamy.

A lifelong activist, Bellamy volunteered for the Peace Corps after college. She later led the pro bono Lawyers Alliance for New York. Bellamy believes that until we deal with domestic violence, "we're not going to build a healthy society." In her opinion, "Everyone has a contribution to make when it comes to helping the less fortunate."

You can be a peacemaker in your community if you try.

Blessed are the peacemakers, for they will be called children of God. (Matthew 5:9)

Guide me in righting wrongs, just Prince of Peace.

Only So Much Time

Stress is on the rise. Personal time is shrinking. Our spirits crave a little peace and quiet.

Let's assume that 8 hours is spent working and 8 sleeping (both points laughable for many these days). That leaves 8 hours for everything else: An hour or so commuting; preparing, eating and cleaning up at least 2 meals a day; buying groceries; paying bills; cleaning house; overseeing homework; taking the youngsters to various practices and meetings; banking; the gas station, the post office, etc., etc.

We're also told to take time daily for time with children; to write in a journal; to exercise; and, to read a newspaper, a chapter of a book and a magazine. And don't forget to pray.

Detach a bit. Think about what really matters. Gain a simpler perspective and choose where you can do less.

Come away to a deserted place...and rest a while. (Mark 6:31)

Jesus, help me make time for myself and for us.

Family Nurturing

Here are a few simple ideas by which families can nurture themselves:

Celebrate special events with foods, customs and rituals that give family members a sense of belonging and a feeling of stability.

Have fun together. Play. Take day trips. Visit a museum.

Contribute to your community's improvement as a family. Volunteer to serve the needy.

Show interest in one another's projects, dreams and struggles. Spend time, especially with each child, listening and encouraging.

Preserve family history, culture and folklore. Assemble family photos and videotapes to share with children and extended family.

Pray together. Cultivating a relationship with the Lord is a family's lifeline to growth in love. Nurturing succeeds when we trust and honor God above all else.

Every member of the family would benefit by taking to heart the parable of the forgiving father and the wayward sons.

I will be the God of all the families. (Jeremiah 31:1)

We are Your family, Lord; love and nurture us.

Surviving a Desert Marathon

Christy Verheul and her trusty steed, Razznan, rode for 21 hours through California's Mojave Desert in the 20 Mule Team endurance horse race. The 100-mile marathon, named after the mule teams that hauled borax from Death Valley, is a test of will. Only about half of the entrants complete it.

They set off at 6 a.m. Nineteen hours later, with rain starting to fall and the other riders far ahead, Verheul began to sing "Raindrops on roses and whiskers on kittens." The song from *The Sound of Music* helped pick up Razznan's pace.

Twenty-six riders finished the race. Verheul, exhausted, sore, and happy was last. Quitting was not an option: "If there's something wrong with the horse, that's one thing. But you don't quit just because you're tired."

We all have days when we feel too tired to go on. Yet, there *is* immense satisfaction in achieving a goal, in crossing a finish line.

You need endurance, so that when you have done the will of God, you may receive what was promised. (Hebrews 10:36)

Holy Spirit, help me to endure to the finish.

A Voice for the Sounds of Silence

Most of the people kidnapped and sold as slaves in the New World passed through what is now Ghana on Africa's Atlantic coast. Visitors today can stand in the dungeons where men, women and children awaited their terrible fate in squalor.

When Renée Kemp went there, she felt the palpable presence of her long-dead slave ancestors.

"Where have you been daughter? There is work to do."

An African-American TV reporter, Ms. Kemp believes her forbearers have called out to her over the centuries to share their stories of horror and brutality, and their feelings of terror, humiliation, despair and anger. So now she is using her writing talent to do just that.

It's up to us, the living, to honor, respect, and remember those who went before us with their lives of tragedy and triumph.

Let us now sing the praises of...our ancestors in their generations. (Sirach 44:1)

God, grant us the strength to seek and share the truth.

A Bit of the Middle East in the U. S.

Ever wonder how a town got its name? When writer and world traveler William Tracy returned to his Southern Illinois hometown after 35 years, he was intrigued by American towns with Middle Eastern names.

He marked towns with a Middle Eastern name on a map and traveled to many of them. He checked libraries for the inspiration behind these names such as geography or climate.

Several cities associated with the Nile River also have homes on the Mississippi River: Memphis, Cairo, Thebes and Karnak. Likewise, the American West, with its deserts, has towns named Baghdad and Mecca. Tracy's research showed that U.S. "towns with Middle Eastern names speak of the daring, industry, faith and fortitude of the nation's early settlers."

What speaks of your faith, fortitude, and daring?

I am going to send an angel in front of you, to guard you on the way and to bring you to the place that I have prepared. (Exodus 23:20)

Father, walk with me as I seek to renew my faith in You.

E-Literature: The Next Wave?

Lately, it seems a controversy is rumbling among writers, publishers and readers alike about the advent of the "e-book," or a book published in digital form rather than with ink on paper.

Critics claim that if the e-book takes over, people will only read popular, condensed works rather than the classics. They believe the e-book signals the death of true literature.

Supporters, however, extol the virtues to be enjoyed: books would cost little or nothing, would never go out of print and would remain available to virtually anyone who is "wired" and connected to the Internet.

Progress can be a subjective thing. What are your views on the ways technology has changed our lives? Has the e-revolution made us more efficient, or has it depersonalized society? Every changing aspect of life deserves scrutiny and serious consideration.

Wisdom is vindicated by all her children. (Luke 7:35)

Jesus, give me the courage to take a stand on issues relevant to our world today.

Master Musician Remembered

In his native New York City, the late band leader Tito Puente is remembered fondly for never forgetting his humble roots.

Important in the fusion of Latin music with jazz, the musician "was a superstar, but he was part of the community," said one local fan upon hearing of his hero's death at age 77. He shared Puente's Puerto Rican heritage and said "You knew that every time you saw him, that for one more day the culture was safe and in good hands."

Louis Bauzo, a musician and teacher, added his perception that the mambo king "was always very accessible to the public." Still another fan, a waitress at Puente's restaurant, said he treated her the same as the well-known musicians and politicians he knew. "He was a beautiful person," she said.

Genuine humility, neither devaluing one's self nor over valuing one's self, is authentic greatness. Cultivate it today.

Wisdom is with the humble. (Proverbs 11:2)

Enable me to love myself as I am, Holy Spirit.

One Life, a Thousand Stories of Courage

Shqipe Malushi could speak only 50 words of English in 1980. This didn't dampen her determination "to learn...English so I could tell the world what was happening to us in Kosovo." When she left for America, she knew her political activism might prevent her return.

She persevered. As political troubles escalated in Kosovo, Malushi's activism intensified. That made political asylum in the United States her only option. She was determined not to waste such a precious gift. Malushi put herself through night school with a series of domestic jobs. Eventually she earned a master's degree in writing. By the 1990s, she was vice president of the public-interest group Albanian American Women's Organization.

Malushi's life is an example of the power of a single individual to overcome, achieve, and succeed through courage, determination and perseverance.

Be brave. (Sirach 19:10)

God, help me find the limitless potential within myself to make a difference.

God: On the Road Again

On her way from Chicago to Georgia to settle her father's estate, Rachel Gold hit a snowstorm in Tennessee. Rachel stopped worrying about how to survive the loss of her father and focused on avoiding an accident. Mile after mile she passed spun-out, abandoned cars.

"These people don't understand snow conditions!" she railed to herself. Half an hour later, she was standing on the shoulder, next to her own totaled rental car. The family in the minivan that picked her up offered her food, a sweater and use of their cell phone. Rachel found herself crying and laughing at the same time. Somewhere between humility, grief, stress and gratitude, Rachel had finally decided to let go and to let God hold her for a while.

Whether He comes in a minivan or a burning bush, we all need to be reminded occasionally that we are still in God's care.

Can a woman forget her nursing child, or show no compassion for the child of her womb?...I will not forget you. (Isaiah 49:15)

Thank You, Jesus, for keeping us in Your loving embrace.

It's Never Too Late

George Dawson gives others hope that growth and change can occur at any age. He has a story to tell about his experiences as a black man in America, including his recollections of older relatives who had been slaves.

Born in a Texas log cabin, Mr. Dawson began work in the fields at age four pressing sugar cane and combing cotton with his grandmother and great-grandmother while listening to their stories.

But Mr. Dawson couldn't have written his story – or read it – until he was 98 years old. That's when he enrolled in an adult literacy program and learned to read. In his "retirement years", Mr. Dawson teamed up with teacher Richard Glaubman to write *Life Is So Good*. He reads his Bible daily and probably doesn't think of himself as inspirational. But he is.

The courage to change is always inspirational.

Do not be afraid; you are of more value than many sparrows. (Luke 12:7)

Show us how to appreciate life, even when it is difficult, Holy Spirit, and how to keep learning and growing.

When Things Change

Change is inevitable, yet often both resisted and welcomed.

There was a time when nurses could easily be identified by the caps they wore along with their crisp white uniforms. Nursing schools designed distinctive headgear which students wore proudly. Some attended "capping ceremonies" held after the successful completion of their first year of study.

Over time, outfits changed for various reasons such as practicality and comfort. Gone were the caps – and even the traditional uniforms. Nurses donned colorful tops with slacks and jogging shoes, or hospital "scrubs."

Initially, patients who had once counted on knowing a nurse by her familiar outfit lamented the changes. It's likely by now most have adjusted. After all, a nurse is still a nurse no matter what she – or he – wears.

While we have to expect change in ourselves and the world around us, there is comfort in recognizing God's unchanging love.

I the Lord do not change. (Malachi 3:6)

Jesus, help us embrace change, and always embrace You.

The Bean that Wakes up the World

"All cares vanish as the coffee cup is raised to the lips." So wrote Sheik Ansari Djezeri Hanball Abdal-Kadir in 1587, centuries before there was a Starbucks.

Long before it was the drink that starts the day for so many, coffee was a food, eaten by nomadic mountain warriors in Ethiopia sometime between 575 and 850. Legend has it that a goatherd named Kaldi noticed that his goats were energized after eating red berries. He tried some and was delighted with the energy surge. A monk noticed Kaldi's habit and boiled the berries to make a drink.

Not all is a "high" in coffee's history. King Charles II's 1675 order closed London coffeehouses for being dens of sedition. In 1777, Frederick the Great denounced coffee in favor of the Prussian national drink, beer. Still today, coffee is, for many, the perfect brew.

History is full of discoveries. Make some for yourself.

Give thanks in all circumstances.
(1 Thessalonians 5:18)

You have given us all good things, Creator. Thank You.

One Woman's Century

At her death in January, 2000, Hazel Wolf had spent a lifetime working against injustices. And she had more time than most for her battles since she was born in the 19th century and died in the 21st.

The 101-year-old resident of Washington State was an environmental activist working for the Audubon Society and other groups for decades. Her interest initially grew out of bird watching, specifically observing a single brown creeper.

Before getting involved in conservation issues, Ms. Wolf had fought for a variety of political and social concerns, starting during the Depression.

We can all work for causes we believe in for whatever time is given us. If something matters to us, it probably matters to others as well. Choose to do good today and every day.

A woman who fears the Lord is to be praised. Give her a share in the fruit of her hands and let her works praise her. (Proverbs 31:30-31)

Inspire women and men who work for justice, Holy Spirit.

Uncommon Wisdom

The British House of Commons is a legislative body renowned the world over for its heated debates on government policy. It was during one such debate in 1926 that Winston Churchill, while defending his proposed budget, passed a bit of leadership wisdom on to members of the House.

It seems Churchill stood accused by a vocal opponent of frequently changing his stance on a particular issue. To this Churchill simply replied, "To improve is to change: to be perfect is to change often."

No one person can know everything or always be right. With those realities we must ultimately be open to other points of view, and more important, be able to admit when we are wrong. In the end, the best leaders are people who can learn from those around them. There's nothing wrong with having an opinion and standing up for what you believe. Just don't be too sure, too fast.

Learn prudence; acquire intelligence.
(Proverbs 8:5)

Teacher, may I humbly hear the voice of others.

Working Out, Doing Chores

An article in *Down East Magazine* titled, "The Maine Workout," discussed the finer points of getting fit while doing daily chores in Maine.

The Snow-Shovel Squat after a Maine nor'easter was praised for priming leg muscles and making triceps bulge. The March Mud-Season Shove to free cars was praised for sculpting leaner thighs.

Leaping up, broom in hand, in the Dust-Web Vertical Leap was said to "make Michael Jordan look like a lead-foot." And the Beer-Can Curl was called "a perfect dumbbell" for shaping the biceps. This can be followed by a jog to the recycling center toting a bag of recyclable items.

Other specifically Maine exercises were recommended, but the message was clear. It is possible to take good care of yourself without a gym membership or fancy gear. Use pesky chores and daily routine to enhance your health. And just as importantly, keep – and exercise – your sense of humor.

Love your neighbor as your self.
(Matthew 19:19)

Creator, remind me that I can not love You or my neighbor, if I do not love my self, and even laugh at myself.

The Driver-Benefactor

Om Dutta Sharma was a practicing lawyer in India. He came to the United States in 1974, unaware that his law degree would mean nothing. An optimistic man, he eventually drove a taxicab in New York City. Yet Sharma leads a second life, that of a philanthropist. When his mother died in 1996, he took the 11,000 rupees she had saved (then about $300) and founded the Ram Kali School for Girls in his hometown.

Sharma and his wife, Krishna, support the school with about $3,000 of their earnings each year. Thanks to them, nearly 200 girls in first through fifth grades are being educated. The school is named for Sharma's mother whom he remembers telling him, "The only thing that cannot be stolen is your education."

As for his own situation, Sharma doesn't hesitate to say that "I am definitely the happiest man in this country."

"It's better to give than to receive" isn't trite. It's true.

A generous person has cause to rejoice. (Sirach 40:14)

Show me the way to true happiness, Lord.

A Role She Can Relish

You remember her as the popular 1970s sitcom star of TV's *Alice*. Now, actress Linda Lavin is perhaps performing her most cherished role ever: as the founder of a theater program that helps young women build self esteem.

Lavin started *Girl Friends,* based in Wilmington, North Carolina, her new home, when she found herself questioning her life and searching for something more. "I was doing show after show (in theater), and coming home each night with a feeling of malaise," she explains. "I thought, is this all there is?"

Lavin decided to dedicate herself to her new community by reaching out to young women who needed to boost their feelings of self worth. Through the program, participants write, direct and perform with Lavin's overall direction and guidance.

What touches your heart? You have more to share than you might realize.

Decide with equity for the meek. (Isaiah 11:4)

Father God, I believe that my decisions and actions define me as a person. Help me stay focused on what matters.

Old and Gray? No Way!

How would you describe the "typical" grandparent these days? The reality of this vibrant generation might surprise you.

According to a 2000 survey by the American Association of Retired Persons (AARP), today's grandparents cite these as their favorite activities with grandkids:

- Eating together, either at home or out
- Shopping for clothes
- Sports, exercise and gardening
- Attending religious services
- Computer activities

As the study reports, today's grandparent is more likely "to be outside playing with a grandchild than inside nodding off while reading." Staying active and interested in others is important not only for older adults, but for the youngsters in their lives.

How attractive is wisdom in the aged.
(Sirach 25:5)

Lord, remind me to respect those older than myself. Help me learn from those who have more experience and a wider perspective than I do.

A Cause to Believe In

On the big screen, Pierce Brosnan stars as James Bond. Between films, Brosnan raises money for women's health causes and environmental preservation because of personal experience. His wife Cassandra died at 39 of ovarian cancer.

Brosnan believes there is a link between health issues and the environment. "The air we breathe and the food we eat sometimes can have disastrous effects on our beings," he says.

Brosnan, who helped start the annual Revlon Run/Walk for Women, feels compelled to help and to care because success as an actor "has to be balanced with giving back to the community."

Regardless of your means or the size of your own community, you have the power to make a commitment to make life better for those in need.

How can you give thanks by giving back?

Be thankful. (Colossians 3:15)

Lord, I pray I will give however and whatever I can.

A Lively Language

Change, we're told, is both life-giving and inevitable. Language is no exception to this rule.

For instance, in the first half of the 20th century people could treat themselves to a meal in an *Automat* rather than opening their *Frigidaires.* Afterwards they might go home and put on the *Victrola* or the *crystal set.* Or they might stop at a *five and ten* or go to a *nickelodeon* or a *talkie.*

By the '60s people, *hippies* and sometimes even *squares, grooved, sat-in,* or *loved-in.* And, of course, *bread* had to be saved for the latest *eight tracks.*

Our language has shifted again. Now there are *lattes* both *short* and *grande.* These fuel *downloads* and *key-ins.* We store information on *zip discs, floppies* and *hard discs.* And on it goes.

Of itself change is neither good nor bad. Go with the flow, holding on to the best; clinging to God.

**Let your speech always be gracious.
(Colossians 4:6)**

Jesus, may I realize that change, gracefully accepted, keeps me vital. Yet help me keep my core values amidst change.

Renewal and Redemption

In 1995, many people believed that America's oldest civil rights group was near-bankrupt and mismanaged beyond repair.

But the NAACP (National Association for the Advancement of Colored People) wasn't washed up. It just needed the strong and determined leadership of someone like human-rights giants Thurgood Marshall or Roy Wilkins.

That leader turned out to be five-term Congressman Kweisi Mfume who left his Maryland legislative seat for the NAACP hot seat. Mfume remembered that "when I was a child, the NAACP was dominant in our community. My mother would pass out literature for them." Under Mfume's leadership, the organization's debt has been erased. He also "wants to create a sense of activism again...Its efforts were never designed to help just blacks; it was designed to make America better."

Every citizen can make his or her country better. It takes hard work and determination. Worthwhile things always do.

There was a disciple...devoted to good works. (Acts 9:36)

Creator, get us past our biases and prejudices.

Local Heroines

Gayle Nikolaisen and her three colleagues at Station 10 in Tacoma, Washington, are an all-female firefighting crew.

The women consider themselves like any other crew, says Nikolaisen. "We're strong, and smart, and we worked way too hard to get here." Tacoma Fire Department Chief Ellen Lewis was the city's first woman firefighter in 1981. Today, 36 of the city's 402 fulltime firefighters are women. Nevertheless, Karen Leming says, "Because we're women, we have to prove we can do this….We're a real team. We trust each other."

The women have the respect of their male peers. 12-year-veteran Paul Sowers says, "There are plenty of calls when a woman can soothe the victim in a way I never could. They just have a way about them."

Women and men aren't inferior or superior to each other; they simply bring different qualities to the job. Let us be thankful we can contribute our unique selves to whatever task is at hand.

God created humankind in His image...male and female He created them. (Genesis 1:27)

We celebrate who and what we are, Creator of all.

Unusual Means of Giving

People find innovative ways to give to good causes.

66-year-old Juergen R. Goldhagen lets his hair grow. "I started to grow it as a lark, but then I realized that by saving on haircuts I could pass those savings on. I save $144 a year. Whenever anyone asks about the ponytail, I tell them, 'It's for *The New York Times* Neediest Cases Fund.'" The Fund supports several established local charities.

Octogenarian Alfred H. Lane walks nearly everywhere he goes and is alert for change and even bills. In a letter with a donation of $482.71, he wrote, "Since the money was found in public areas, I would like it to be used to help...the homeless." Eleanor H. Watts eliminated "one coffee to go" a day and sent a check for $30. John and Eleanor Fischer sent a check for $230 in honor of the 230 victims of T.W.A. Flight 800.

Giving is its own gift. What can you do with your spare change? ...if you dig a little deeper?

God loves a cheerful giver. (2 Corinthians 9:7)

Help me, Generous Lord, find ways to help the needy.

Ming the Wanted

When Rose Lewis adopted a Chinese baby, she did not know it would lead her to becoming an author. *I Love You Like Crazy Cakes* became a children's picture-book bestseller. Lewis, a TV news producer, wrote the book both as a gift for her daughter, Ming, and to let her and other adopted youngsters know how much they are wanted.

She had always hoped to marry and have children. But as Lewis approached 40, and a long-term relationship came apart, she decided: "I can't do anything about my love life. But I can do something about being a mother."

Today, though single motherhood is a struggle, Lewis says, "I don't know what I'd do without Ming." She's also delighted that her book has convinced some readers to adopt children.

Some choices can surprise us with the joy they bring.

Let the little children come to Me; do not stop them; for it is to such as these that the kingdom of God belongs. (Mark 10:14)

Father, may I be fearless in finding and giving love.

Dungeon Doors

Winston Churchill, Prime Minister of Great Britain during World War II, tried to encourage his fellow citizens in some dark times. Here's one brief tale he told: "Remember the story of the Spanish Prisoner. For many years he was confined in a dungeon…One day it occurred to him to push the door of his cell. It was open; and it had never been locked."

Often we are like the Spanish prisoner. We may resign ourselves to our "fate" rather than take responsibility for our predicament. We may have been handed a bad situation but we are also graced with the ability to make it better.

Some barriers are only made of excuses or a lack of confidence. They may be easier to cross than we think – if we try. Like the prisoner, we may find that our own dungeons have been locked by our fears – but will open with the key of hope.

Hope that is seen is not hope. …But if we hope for what we do not see, we wait for it with patience. (Romans 8:24,25)

Jesus, may I never be confined by my own resignation.

Sweet Treat

Kay Allenbaugh has compiled a series of books including *Chocolate for a Woman's Spirit* featuring stories of inspiration. One of the contributors is Sue Dyer, who has watched her career grow from secretary to executive director, editor, and, in her own words, "holder of a reputation for being able to do the impossible."

Her secret? Acting as if.

Along the way, she learned she would find success if she acted as if she were already the person she longed to be. "By acting as if," she writes, "...The law of cause and effect will eventually move me where I desire to be." Sue sees God's hand in the process: "I act as if and tap into the infinite source of good. He always gives me what I need and desire, and so much more!"

Trust God and He will give you your heart's desire.

O Lord...give success to Your servant today. (Nehemiah 1:11)

Holy God, let us approach Your throne with the confident knowledge that we are Your beloved children.

Dancing without Fear

Judith Jameson, artistic director of the Alvin Ailey American Dance Theater, spent her first six years with the company in relative obscurity. Then Ailey created a demanding ballet for her, *Cry,* as a gift to his mother.

When it was over, she expected to continue in anonymity. But *The New York Times* proclaimed, "The Dance: Judith Jameson's Triumph." As the weight of the review began to sink in, fear gripped her. She knew that as she danced again that evening, people would be paying closer attention. Finally, Jameson realized that before the review, she had felt she was just doing her job. "The only difference was that somebody had recognized my work," she observed. With that freeing thought, she fearlessly took the stage again and again.

Don't let fear paralyze you. Do what you have to do.

There is a season and a time for every matter under heaven. (Ecclesiastes 3:1)

Lord, let me embrace Your gifts and follow Your way, unconcerned about the judgments of others.

Morality 101

You are not likely to see a course in "doing the right thing" as part of most high school curriculums.

But when students at Townsend Harris High in Queens, New York were asked to write about moral choices they had to make in their own lives, the students responded with fervor. The best essays were entered in a citywide contest.

Eight students from Townsend Harris took home more prizes than those from the other 48 participating schools. José Melendez won second prize for recounting an emotional episode in which he intervened in another teen's life. Michael Berger, another Townsend student, took third place for his account of how he risked his friends' scorn for aiding a homeless man.

Moral choices confront each one of us every day. Think about some difficult choices you have made. Would you make those choices today? ...or act differently?

Decide with equity. (Isaiah 11:4)

Give me the courage, Spirit of Wisdom, to be honest with myself.

To Life!

One episode of the television series *Frasier* opens with the characters returning from a funeral. Frasier's father has been given a bottle of wine by the man's widow. A friend laments: "He probably waited his whole life for an occasion special enough to open that bottle."

It's a good reminder to not only live in the present, but to live there fully. There will always be deadlines and obligations. Will the world stop if you put off those phone calls until tomorrow and opt, instead, to enjoy the evening with your children? To take a walk with your spouse or closest friend? To visit with a dear friend after too long an absence?

Do not put off joy. Instead, resolve, today, to live life now.

All to whom God gives wealth and possessions and whom He enables to enjoy them, and to...find enjoyment in their toil–this is the gift of God. (Ecclesiastes 5:19)

Give me the courage to seize the moment with gusto, Lord!

A New Spirit in the Air?

Are we becoming more spiritually minded?

On the eve of the year 2000, David Gergen wrote in *U. S. News & World Report:* "Americans are hungering for something more than money and a new car. They are looking for answers that satisfy the soul and restore a sense of belonging to one another."

Using as a guide five areas covered in the *Index of Leading Cultural Indicators,* Gergen cites what he sees as positive trends.

Crime – the national rate has declined for seven years in a row

Family – abortion is down; divorce rates lower

Education – the "standards" movement is catching on

Youth – teen pregnancy and drug use are down

Religion – charitable giving is up; people talk about God

How do things look in your community? In your home?

If you wish to enter into life, keep the commandments. (Matthew 19:17)

Be with us, God, in our lifelong journey.

Brave Conductors on Underground Railroad

Racism is born of hatred and fear. The Underground Railroad, a network of safe havens for runaway slaves on their journey to freedom, was born of courage and risk-taking on the part of enslaved Americans as well as those who helped them.

Many white women, often without their husbands' knowledge, took risks "letting escaped slaves come into their homes and making sure food was available to them," according to Anita Dixon-Andrews of Passages Unlimited Inc., a Kansas tour company specializing in African-American historical sites. She says these women were among the many unsung heroes of the Underground Railroad.

The Underground Railroad was also a system of education, according to Ms. Dixon-Andrews. Those traveling its path were guided by the stars. They also learned about plants known to be good for healing or eating.

Hatred and prejudice still exist. The personal courage to combat these evils are needed more than ever.

For freedom Christ has set us free. (Galatians 5:1)

Father, give good people the courage to do great things.

Mr. Lincoln on Government

In his inaugural address of March 4, 1861 Abraham Lincoln noted that the U.S. had been formed "by the Articles of Association of 1774" and that "perpetuity is implied...in the fundamental law of all national governments." He added that the U.S. "with its institutions, belongs to the" inhabitants.

He called citizens the president's "rightful masters." And said that the president "derives all his authority from the people...His duty is to administer the present Government as it came to his hands and to transmit it unimpaired...to his successor."

Lincoln added, "Why should there not be a patient confidence in the ultimate justice of the people? ...While the people retain their virtue and vigilance no Administration...can very seriously injure the Government."

Be informed. Be involved. Put Abraham Lincoln's words on citizenship into action.

Do good; seek justice, rescue the oppressed, defend the orphan, plead for the widow. (Isaiah 1:17)

Inspire and inform my citizenship, Holy Spirit.

Modern-day Scribes

On the first Ash Wednesday of the new millennium, Welsh calligrapher Donald Jackson began the daunting task of creating the first handwritten, illuminated Bible since the invention of the printing press over 500 years ago. Over the next four years, Jackson and his team of calligraphers plan to hand-letter a seven volume, 1,150 page Bible.

However, there are modern twists: The font designed for the Bible has been digitized to allow the calligraphers to copy from a computer-generated template or layout of each page.

The combination of ancient craftsmanship and contemporary tools will provide a valuable record of the way the Bible has been interpreted and applied in our time. For Jackson and his fellow scribes, this labor of love provides a unique and inspired way to impart the word of God.

How do you impart God's Good News?

All scripture is inspired by God and is useful for teaching, for reproof, for correction, and for training in righteousness. (1 Timothy 3:16)

In the beginning and evermore, the Word is You, Lord.

Taking Time for Gratitude

Jeannette Kennedy Baldridge of Maine recalls the night she and her husband Donnie learned to more fully appreciate their lives. Donnie was more than three hours late coming home from work. When he did, Jeannette knew by the look on his face that something terrible had happened.

Donnie had seen a fellow motorist killed in a collision with a moose. And he and another driver had waited for the police to arrive at the accident scene. Accidents such as this were not rare in Maine in the spring, but it was sobering to see up close.

Donnie and Jeannette realized how close he had come to being the one who had had the fatal accident; the preciousness of each moment of their lives; "how often we go through our days preoccupied with unimportant things, oblivious to the miracle of all our perfectly wonderful, ordinary days."

Consider the beauty in a friend's wave, a child's giggle, a rainbow; a meal. Savoring the beauty in life's everyday moments is a worthy challenge.

Give thanks. (2 Chronicles 20:21)

Accept my deep gratitude for every moment, Creator.

Minding Everyone's Ps & Qs

She may be over 80 years old, but when it comes to details, don't mess with Eleanor Gould Packard, who has worked as the grammarian for *The New Yorker* magazine for 52 years.

Her desk seems in danger of buckling under the weight of paper, manuscripts and books. Behind it she sits, pencil in hand, working her way down seemingly endless columns of type. Her quarry is linguistic sloppiness, ambiguity, redundancy, dangling modifiers, disagreeing pronouns, mixed metaphors and the like.

While Gould Packard's name is not quite as recognizable as, Harold Ross, E. B. White or William Shawn (founders of the magazine), she has been responsible for much of the magazine's style. In certain circles, Gould Packard is a legend, referred to as the "Orwell of copy editors."

When success is the result of a collaborative effort, a less visible contributor is sometimes overlooked. Try to appreciate and thank all who deserve it.

Human success is in the hand of the Lord. (Sirach 10:5)

Jesus, help me strive for excellence in my work.

Going Against the Grain

As recently as the 1950s, the powerfully destructive screwworm threatened American livestock.

It was Dr. Edward Knipling, a government entomologist, who began work on obliterating the now little-remembered menace. The striped, grayish insect was, at that time, the scourge of farmers in the South. The parasitic insect would attack full-grown cattle, which would then often die within days.

Although some regarded his efforts which focused on sterilization rather than the use of pesticides as unconventional, Dr. Knipling persevered. Today, the pest is no longer a threat here.

Popular causes are easy to follow. But beliefs that are not "mainstream" or "current" are not. Look at these as ways way to strengthen character and perseverance.

Let us run with perseverance the race set before us. (Hebrews 12:1)

Jesus, You are a living example of going against the grain. Help me follow You in my heart and in my actions.

One Big Happy Family

Newspapers and television seem to be filled with dysfunctional families. Is that all there are?

Not really. Many families manage to be happy. In fact, many parents and kids really enjoy being with each other. Their secret? Interviews with "happy families" point to the following:

- They talk: no matter how difficult the subject or how raw the emotions, and they listen to one another.
- They fight fairly: no name-calling, no dredging up past issues, no belittling the other's position.
- They make time to be a family.
- They realize that no one outgrows the need for love and affection.
- They all contribute to the household.
- They respect each other's privacy and property.
- They stress the positive.

Every family can be a happy one.

Let us work for the good of all, and especially for those of the family of faith. (Galatians 6:10)

Help us, Father, Your sons and daughters, to love You and one another.

Not Finishing What You Started

From the earliest days of childhood, we hear the message that good things come only to those who persevere. Keep at every task until it's finished, we're told. "A winner never quits, and a quitter never wins," we hear.

Well, maybe not. As the century ended, the *Wall Street Journal* reported the national "quit rate"—people who voluntarily left their last jobs—was 14.5 percent, the highest since the late 1980s. While no one is advocating giving up at the first sign of difficulty, it is sometimes good to quit. Finishing what you started is useful only if what you started is worth finishing.

And often you don't know whether it's worth finishing until after you have started. Of course, there should be serious thought behind stopping a course of action, including reasons that point to personal or family safety and sanity. In those cases, then, whether it's a job or a path in life, it's okay to stop before you're finished.

Abide in Me as I abide in you. (John 15:4)

Be with me, Lord, help me as I work through each day.

An Attitude for Thanks

Do you feel life has treated you badly or unfairly?

Maybe it's time to change your attitude to one of gratitude. "Having a positive attitude is essential," a reader from Ohio wrote to *Modern Maturity* magazine. "I am very grateful for life and just to be alive."

Says another from New Jersey: "All my life I have fought the battle of low self-esteem. I fight the insecurities and never stop trying. And when I am at my lowest, I enumerate all the things I am thankful for."

More people need to do the same, instead of wasting time reaffirming bad memories, self-described failures and past moments of shame. Such actions only boost negativity – and bring you down.

Feeling grateful is good for you and those around you. Expressing gratitude allows us to reach out in love and share happiness. Start saying "thank you" more often.

Sing to the Lord with thanksgiving. (Psalm 147:7)

Thank You, Father, for Your unconditional love for me.

Story with a Happy Ending

Kim Gosselin vividly remembers the February Saturday when her life changed forever. Her son Jayson was sick again, not with the flu, as the doctors had thought, but with diabetes. Kim and her husband Gary learned about the disease from hospital staff. But when Kim searched for answers in print that would help Jayson understand, she came up empty.

Kim decided to write about the subject herself. Together, the Gosselins published a book on diabetes. And when their other son, Justin, developed asthma, the couple published a book on that topic as well. In fact, they have published books on several children's health issues and even started a foundation to fund research into cures for the illnesses the books address.

"I really believed God had given us this situation so we could help others," Kim says. "I would give anything in the world for Jayson not to have diabetes, but I try to remember that without it, I couldn't have helped...other children and their families."

Pursue justice. (Sirach 27:8)

You are with us, always, Master, source of all joy and all strength.

Monks Who Fight Fires

Bitter cold temperatures, high winds, snow - an ordinary winter's day in Minnesota. Walking from one building to the next on the campus of St. John's University in Collegeville can literally freeze your face.

On this January morning, Brother Bradley Jenniges rushes out into the cold to fight a fire. The Benedictine monks of St. John's are all about service – to God, to their students and to the community. For more than 60 years, the monks have protected the campus, acting as the first line of defense against fires and other emergencies. They train monthly, preparing for different aspects of the job. Daily, there is still plenty of time for prayer.

"Sometimes when the pager goes off at 2 a.m., it's not any fun," Brother Bradley says. "But people on campus are glad we're here. There is a need for us to fulfill this role."

The Lord has many important roles for us to fill.

I want you to understand this mystery. (Romans 11:25)

Fill me with Your Spirit, Lord, so that I may set the world on fire with Your love.

Nursery Rhymes – Not Always Kid Stuff

Things aren't always what they seem.

Take some of today's innocent and happy nursery rhymes, for example. In the beginning *Humpty Dumpty* wasn't a fantasy egg sitting on a wall. This rhyme is thought to refer to an unfortunate nobleman who fell out of favor with King Richard III.

Ring Around the Rosey didn't start out as a charming children's poem. It began as a street song about the Great Plague in London which killed 70,000 people between 1664 and 1665. Victims saw the rosy rash first – and later "all fall down."

In her book, *Accidents May Happen,* Charlotte Foltz Jones reveals more stories behind the stories. "Some began as folk songs or ballads sung in taverns. ...Some rhymes were written to poke fun" at the powerful.

The simplest things may not be quite so simple after all.

Never speak against the truth. (Sirach 4:25)

God, may we find true meaning in life.

"Mom Really Mattered"

At 83, Agnes Jones still walked miles up and down Main Street visiting shops and friends almost every day, but when she died one winter, neither of her daughters expected her last wish to be so surprising. "I was shocked, at first," says Ellen, the elder of the two. "It was unlike anything I'd ever heard of." Her sister, Dot, agrees. Their mother had requested that she be cremated and that her ashes be scattered up and down Main Street.

"It seemed ghoulish, disrespectful," Dot explains, "until the service, when the hundreds of people she said hello to daily came up to my sister and me and told us what a loss they felt. Mom really mattered to all of them."

Dot adds, "Honoring Mom's request was the 'happiest sad' I've even been, but now she's right there for us every day and night, smiling from her favorite places with her good friends. What a lesson!"

Whatever your faith tradition, remember and honor those who have gone before you

Imitate what is good. (3 John 11)

Help me to make each life I touch better, and help me to touch many, Jesus.

Virtues for Every One

Poverty. Chastity. Obedience. The three vows of a consecrated life sound difficult, if not impossible to many people. But Sister Deborah Cerullo, S.S.N.D. believes that the virtues behind these vows can help us draw closer to God and make sense of our lives.

"The vows of poverty, chastity and obedience are not ends in themselves, says Sister Deborah. "Things, people and control over the conditions of our lives are often blessings. Poverty in itself is an evil to be eradicated. Chastity, living out one's sexuality according to one's state in life, can be cold and distancing if lived without love. Obedience without freedom is domination. ..."

But "when we can say that our fundamental security lies not in wealth, or another person, or power, but rather in God, then we are living the virtues of the religious vows."

Ask yourself whether these virtues are part of your life.

Strive first for the kingdom of God and His righteousness. (Matthew 6:33)

You are all I need, Adorable, Merciful God.

Forgive and (Sort of) Forget?

Most of us have heard the expression, "Forgive and forget." Yet, when life presents us with an opportunity to do it, it isn't that easy.

Dr. Richard Winters says, "Forgiveness is offering someone a gift and releasing them from a debt." That's easy to read about in a novel or the Gospels; hard to practice.

How can we become more forgiving? Music industry executive Jackie Patillo says forgiveness "is not holding someone to account for a wrong they've done to you." She adds that forgiveness is incomplete if "you're still holding a grudge or you're thinking differently of a person who has...hurt you."

According to publicist Susan Coker many practice "shallow forgiveness....We don't really look at how someone has hurt us or sinned against us. We quickly say, 'Oh, I forgive you,' without acknowledging the depth and pain."

Have you done your emotional housecleaning; forgiving those who have hurt you?

Forgive us our debts, as we also have forgiven our debtors. (Matthew 6:12)

Jesus, be my example of perfect forgiveness.

Economics of Compassion

John Kenneth Galbraith is known as the "people's economist." He has taught at Harvard University for over fifty years and has served as an advisor to a host of American Presidents. He is most famous for his part in creating the "New Deal" program with Franklin Delano Roosevelt. This plan helped millions of depression-era Americans get on their feet again.

But the gaps between rich and poor are widening. Why? Mr. Galbraith says, "Unquestionably, 50 years ago people were more generous because there were more people who were in need themselves. As people have escaped personal need, they have escaped the problems of those who are still in it."

While sympathy and understanding come more easily through shared experiences, we should also strive to recognize the needs of those with whom we might not identify so readily. Give whole-heartedly of whatever your gifts may be and you will find that your compassion will bless your own soul.

Help the poor for the commandment's sake. (Sirach 29:9)

Lord, may I see You in needy women, children and men.

Five Dollars and a Dream

In 1935 Llewellyn Scott heard Catholic activist Dorothy Day speak about works of mercy. Impressed by Day's accomplishments in housing, feeding and caring for the poor, Scott asked Day how he, too, could open a house of hospitality. "Just start doing it," Day said, "and here's $5 – it's all I have."

Scott accepted the startup money and began his own house of hospitality, living and working for Washington D.C.'s poor for nearly four decades.

Perhaps most important, Scott began his work when the effects of the Great Depression were hitting people hardest. Those nearby who were homeless, jobless, hungry and without hope could find some relief, thanks to Scott's faith and dedication.

People like Llewellyn Scott show that opportunities for goodness and holiness lie in the bleakest of circumstances.

Every good tree bears good fruit. (Matthew 7:17)

Holy Spirit, I pray that with Your guidance and comfort, I am better able to see the positive possibilities in all situations.

Name that Tulip

Apricot Beauty...Angelique...Queen of the Night. No, make that Queen of Night.

As aficionados know, tulip names have two words, sometimes three; never four. "Yet even some high-profile catalogs list it that way," says Sally Ferguson, with the Netherlands Flower Bulb Information Center in Brooklyn, New York.

Tulips come in many different colors, combinations and designs. Some well-known people have a tulip named after them. "Christening" a flower is an event. It means that a tulip is unique in some way. With christening comes a permanent place in the international register of tulip names.

"Having a tulip named for one is quite an honor," says Holly Coors, matriarch of the brewing family and tulip lover. The entire process, from seed to bulb to sale can take years.

Even people who know nothing about tulip names enjoy their beauty. God's beautiful creation is truly boundless.

From the greatness and beauty of created things comes a corresponding perception to their Creator. (Wisdom of Solomon 13:5)

Teach us, Lord, to appreciate the beauties of nature.

Leadership 101

Every successful follower is at times a leader; every successful leader, a follower. The executive is the mother of several children. Weekends or evenings, the entrepreneur becomes an expert with fabrics, water temperatures, detergent and bleach and ironing. So a leader is, firstly, a servant. But a leader also...

- does what is right, not what is popular.
- is genuinely interested in others
- is always growing
- is a person of honesty and integrity who admits personal failures
- makes others better
- begins a project before success is certain
- is quick to praise and encourage the smallest improvement

Is your leadership style modeled on Jesus'? You, your friends, neighbors and associates, the world, can use all the service and leadership you have.

Whoever wishes to be great among you must be your servant. (Matthew 20:26)

Servant Lord, bless us with wise political leaders.

Beginning Anew

Thinking about that second (or third) career, but also thinking you might be too old?

Joe McMahon was a successful New York advertising executive. He also soared in his second career as an executive recruiter. But he still dreamed of becoming a published songwriter. In his 20s, he had written several ballads, hoping one day his work would be published.

Nearly 60 years later his dream was realized. At age 83 he released his first compact disk, *Second Hand Heart for Sale*. It contained eight of the songs he had written 60 years before.

There are others who, like McMahon, refuse to let age or the passage of time deter them from following a dream. Researcher Lydia Bronte says it is typical for high-achievers once retired to "feel free to do what they wanted." It really is never too late to begin anew. Age is a state of mind.

A blameless life is ripe old age. (Wisdom 4:9)

Creator, instill in me a respect for the elderly and all they have experienced and accomplished in life.

The Path Least Imagined

When Wilfried Hoffman was a young German exchange student in the United States, a brush with death in a car accident prompted the attending physician to remark, "God must have something special in mind for you."

Hoffman left the U.S. and soon forgot the incident. But in 1980, after much reading and reflection, the scholar with two graduate degrees and years of service in the German diplomatic corps made a life-changing decision: He converted to Islam.

While the conversion was difficult for his peers to accept, Hoffman fulfilled his commitments and eventually retired from service. He now writes and travels ceaselessly, seeking to explain Muslims and Christians to one another.

The path to a life of service is often unpredictable, difficult, and sometimes, unpopular. Whatever niche, usual or unusual, that you are called to fill, it is worthwhile and needed in God's eyes.

Commit your work to the Lord. (Proverbs 16:3)

Remind me daily, Lord, that I am here for a purpose, for a unique and special calling.

Suffer the Little Children

The United Nations declares that the least powerful, least prestigious and least important among us had rights. The *Convention on the Rights of the Child* says that each child has the right to:

- protection from war
- protection from violence
- adequate nutrition
- health care and vaccination
- free primary education
- a family and home
- protection from forced labor
- equal opportunity regardless of gender or race or ethnicity

On reflection, these are the bare minimums for a human life for children and adults, young and old alike. But can adults expect to enjoy them if they don't first extend these rights to children?

Whoever welcomes one such child in My name welcomes Me. (Matthew 18:4-5)

Children are Your gift to the world, Abba. Help us respect children, their needs, their innate dignity, their rights.

Batter Up...for Everybody!

Beth Campbell couldn't stand to watch her son, Stevie, miss out on the fun of baseball because of his handicaps. So she created "Buddy Ball."

In the game, physically and mentally challenged youngsters are paired with normally developed older kids who do for their partners the throwing, running or hitting they can't do for themselves. Everyone plays and wears team uniforms. Innings end only when the full batting order is complete. No score is kept.

In other words, everybody plays and everybody wins.

Campbell says the game gives challenged kids "a chance to be part of the regular gang... (and it) spurs them to strive harder to reach their maximum abilities, however limited those may be."

"I saw my kids learn true compassion and experience a ball game...played for fun, not for winning," says one mother.

Compassion is a good reason to do anything.

Provoke one another to love and good deeds. (Hebrews 10:24)

Each of us, Father, has a unique way to serve You. Help us to know it this day.

Dumping on History

The rich red Alabama soil that marks the land along the highway that stretches from Selma to Montgomery is also rich in history. In March 1965, it was here, along Highway 80, that a 54-mile march between those two Alabama cities led to the passage of the 1965 Voting Rights Act.

The local black farmers let the marchers camp overnight on their land. And along this road, black sharecroppers, evicted for daring to register to vote, built a settlement named Tent City.

This same highway is now targeted as a landfill, with developers citing the ideal tightly packed clay soil. Those in favor of that idea tout the creation of jobs and revenue for Lowndes County where 40 percent of the 13,000 residents live below the poverty level. Still there are many crying "foul" to the plan to dump on this national historic trail.

Balancing today's needs with appreciation for the past requires wisdom. Strive to be wise in all your choices.

For freedom Christ has set us free. (Galatians 5:1)

At all times, You are with us, Master. Give us the wisdom to know Your will.

Tomorrow's Children

David and Alice Jurist are long-time supporters of the Hackensack (New Jersey) University Medical Center for the treatment and cure of children with life-threatening diseases. At a building dedication ceremony, the Jurists, whose daughter Eileen survived Hodgkin's disease, said, "The work...to help find a cure for cancer will only end when no parent will lose the promise of tomorrow."

12,500 children and young adults under the age of 21 are diagnosed with cancer each year. The 70 percent who are cured represent a substantial improvement, but it's not enough for people like the Jurists.

Their daughter Eileen said, "The future should never be constrained by the limits of today, but must be built on the hopes of tomorrow."

Every human being thrives on hope, especially children. Do all you can to give them a chance.

Hope does not disappoint us. (Romans 5:5)

Child Jesus, may all children enjoy a healthy tomorrow.

The Self-Control Muscle

Psychological experiments conducted by Mark Muravan and researchers at Case Western Reserve University conclude that our willpower is as susceptible to fatigue as are muscles during exercise. Willpower is limited. Multiple challenges, temptations and stresses all seem to deplete the same basic source of energy. This suggests that writing a list of New Year's resolutions likely spreads our willpower too thin. And major life changes such as a new baby or a new job may weaken self-control in other areas.

The research also indicates that self-control gets stronger with use but fades with disuse. So besides those daily workouts at the gym, exercise that self-control as well.

Toning our character along with our biceps puts us in top moral shape.

Support your faith with goodness...knowledge...self-control...endurance...godliness and...mutual affection. (2 Peter 1:5,6)

Help me resist temptations against faith, Holy Spirit.

Saving Dying Languages

Berty Segal Cook is a noted language consultant who helps rescue dying languages and, in the process, preserve cultures that might otherwise disappear.

The seventeen bands of the Shuswap Nation, for instance, determined in 1982 to preserve their language and with it their history and culture. Working with a group of women on the Shuswap Reserve in British Columbia, Ms. Cook uses a lively teaching technique called "Total Physical Response."

More and more native peoples want to preserve their languages and pass them on to the younger generation. It isn't an easy task. English is pervasive and available teachers and courses are limited. Still, the effort shows some signs of success. Students registering for a second language in local public schools have a choice of either French or Secwepemctsin, the Shuswap native tongue.

Language is a great gift. Respect your own and others'.

King Darius wrote to all peoples and nations of every language...tremble and fear before the God of Daniel. (Daniel 6:25,26)

God, help us value the language and culture of other people.

Pianos and People: a Beautiful Match

Pianos have become so much a part of everyday life that it's hard to imagine a time without them.

Nevertheless, the piano wasn't invented until about 1700, in Italy by Bartolomeo Cristofori. The piano has been not only a musical instrument but also a work of art, a welcome piece of furniture and even a status symbol.

In the hands of major concert pianists as well as rock musicians, the piano has afforded countless listeners hours of pleasure.

In fact, the piano holds such appeal that adults who struggled over lessons as children hold out a secret hope that with enough practice they, too, can make a bit of musical magic with their fingers and those ivory and black keys.

Make an added effort to appreciate the beauty of music in your own life.

A seal of emerald in a rich setting of gold is ...music with good wine. (Sirach 32:5)

Thank You, Lord, for the music that enriches our days.

Pooling in Order to Serve

Basketball may define most of the Hoosier State, but swimming rules in the town of Carmel. Their girls' team has won its fourteenth straight title; the boys' teams three state titles. Much of this success is attributed to Coach Tony Young.

Coach Young says, "They're very hardworking, goal-oriented kids. Swimmers take lessons from the school's current stars. They talk a lot about tradition and believing in yourself. Our leaders continue to be leaders years after they graduate."

Past and present team members offer ideas for service and Young supports their interests. The club has joined the Making Waves swim-a-thon, to benefit the Indiana Blind Children's Foundation at the suggestion of alumna Kim Broad. She says, "This is our way to give back to the community."

We are all blessed in so many ways. It's up to each of us to find a way to give back to our communities.

The fruits of the spirit are peace, patience, kindness, generosity. (Galatians 5:22)

Spirit of Love, inspire me to be liberal in my contributions to others.

Caring for All the Children

When Emmy winner Susan Lucci gave birth to her son, Andreas, he was in intensive care with a viral infection for a month. "I remember the neonatologist saying, 'Never underestimate the power of talking to your baby and holding his hand. ...This gives him strength.'"

Today, Andreas is fully recovered and in college. His mom, now a spokesperson for the March of Dimes, says, "when your baby is in a life-threatening situation, it's to hell and back for all of you. My heart goes out to the babies and the parents."

Lucci also supports Little Flower Children's Services of New York, a foster care and adoption services agency. Susan Lucci's actions reflect her commitment and devotion to the cause of maternal and infant welfare.

Do your commitments reflect a devotion to a worthwhile cause? Share yourself with people in need.

Can a woman forget her nursing child, or show no compassion for the child of her womb? Even these may forget, yet I will not forget you. (Isaiah 49:15)

Show us how to care for each other, loving Father.

Inventors: a Hardy Breed

The world of inventors and inventions is not for the faint of heart. Raymond Damadian went through a lot before receiving recognition for his project. His invention, a whole-body scanner called the Indomitable "represents a milestone in the history of medical imaging," according to Smithsonian magazine.

The effort to find a better method by which doctors could examine their patients' inner workings would lead to today's rather commonplace magnetic resonance machines (MRIs).

But for Damadian the quest was filled with obstacles including the doubts of those who thought his idea farfetched. At one point, he even acted as his own guinea pig. In 1989 he was inducted into the National Inventors Hall of Fame in Ohio for his contributions to MRI technology.

Inspiration, hard work and plenty of time are usually the right mix for success.

Bear fruit with patient endurance. (Luke 8:15)

Inspire and encourage me, Savior.

Things We Take for Granted

Essential yet often ignored and taken for granted? Overworked and under appreciated? At this point, many parents, employees and others might be nodding their heads in recognition.

However, what science is referring to as something we can't live without and which we often overlook is the colorless, odorless and gaseous nitrogen.

Nitrogen is found in the cells of every living thing. It actually makes up 80 percent of the air we breathe, though we merely breathe it back out again. Vital to the cycle of life, nitrogen plays an important role in maintaining the biosphere.

Lots of things are easy to ignore, but that does not mean it's wise or prudent to do so. Be willing to pay attention to your world.

Have your lamps lit; be like those who are waiting for their master to return from the wedding banquet. (Luke 12:35-36)

Open our eyes to the signs of Your immanence, Jesus.

Build Your Relationship with God

Mitchel Perry is a self-improvement author who writes about making the most of situations like work, family and even conflict. Four words he suggests applying to any situation are: Ritualize, Visualize, Optimize and Capitalize.

Could these also apply to your relationship with God?

- Worship and prayer are traditional rituals passed on from the Lord Himself.
- By visualizing your relationship with Him growing stronger, you will learn the road to strengthening it.
- Your faith, in trying times, can be optimized by knowing and relying on His loving wisdom.
- What better cause for celebration than knowing you are growing closer to the Lord and all He wants for you?

Think about your relationship with God. Pay the same attention to it as you do to the other relationships in your life.

Love the Lord. (Psalm 31:23)

Show me how to love You more fully every day, Christ.

Why Lettuce and Money are the Same Color

You could pay up to $40 for a simple green salad, if you want to eat it at "the right" restaurant and be seen with a certain class of society. Or not.

The rest of us probably have other plans for dinner and our budget. Plus, while salad can be tasty and good for you, remember that food is fuel. Consider the following list of high energy foods:

Yogurt; Cheese; Bananas; Turkey; Eggs

Each of these all-natural delicacies comes from a far greater and less-exclusive provider than any restaurant. The Lord has been supplying them in abundance since the Garden of Eden.

It is easy to overcomplicate the simple blessings all around us. Consider His intentions as you view the world.

All look to You to give them their food in due season; when You give to them, they gather it up...they are filled with good things.
(Psalm 104:27-28)

You provide enough bounty so that none should want, Lord. Teach us to share with all our brothers and sisters.

Remembering a Famine

Reports of potatoes going black in some fields in Ireland came in 1845. What was dismissed as "just a bad year" was followed in 1846 and again in 1847 by the loss of three quarters of the crop. A Peruvian potato fungus had planted itself deeply and disastrously in the Irish soil.

At the time, 75 percent of Ireland's people relied heavily on the potato as their main food source. The Great Famine of 1845-1850 turned Ireland into a land overrun with death and disease. One and a half million people died; 1,200,000 fled their native land.

Ireland's former president, Mary Robinson, has said of the Famine: "Let us not be prisoners of our history. The best possible commemoration of the men and women who died in that Famine, who were cast up on other shores because of it, is to take their dispossession into the a present with us, to help others who now suffer in similar way." A history lesson, indeed.

The alien who resides with you shall be to you as the citizen...love the alien as yourself. (Leviticus 19:34)

Give me courage, Father, and strength to face all trials.

Expanding Horizons

When James R. Langevin was elected to the U.S. House of Representatives in November, 2000, Congress wasn't quite ready for him. As the first paraplegic member of the House, the Rhode Islander could not use the Congressional men's room or the phones in the cloakroom. The chamber required renovations to accommodate those who use wheelchairs.

"Jim is carrying the crusade I began in the Senate to the House," said Senator Max Cleland, a triple amputee from Georgia. "For the first six months I was in the Senate, I had to use the ladies room."

Langevin, who had a freak accident at age 16, expects to advocate for those with disabilities. "I understand the nature of disabilities probably more than most because I am disabled." But there are many issues he wants to work on. "Being disabled is part of who I am, but it doesn't define me."

What defines you? How do you define yourself?

You shall not revile the deaf or put a stumbling block before the blind...I am the Lord. (Leviticus 19:14)

Remind us, Creator, that we are all disabled in one way or another, visibly or invisibly.

Cairo's Consummate Café

When al-Fishawy began serving coffee to his friends in an alleyway in his native Cairo almost 250 years ago, little did he know then that his café would still be around in the 21st century.

Fishawy's stands today as a cramped, noisy and enormously popular gathering place in the hub of Cairo's richest area of Islamic architecture and historic sites. Perhaps because of its location, or maybe simply the good fare and atmosphere, Fishawy's has served as a favorite hangout for more than two centuries of Egyptian writers, musicians, students and intellectuals. As one frequent patron says, "I like it because people from all classes come here. It has a harmonious feel."

Traveling to other parts of the world makes us realize how small the world really is. More importantly, we can see how similar people from different countries really are.

The Lord said to Abram...in you all the families of the earth shall be blessed. (Genesis 12:1,3)

Lord, inspire me to learn about Your world and its people.

Pictures Tell the Story

In the beginning there was the Word. As illustrator Barry Moser knows, the pictures must follow, but are sometimes just as memorable.

A celebrated book illustrator for years, Moser's latest project is perhaps his grandest: a fully illustrated version of the King James Bible, marking the first time a major artist has illustrated the complete texts of both the Old and New Testaments since 1865. It is called the Pennyroyal Caxton Bible.

The one-time Methodist preacher returned to the words themselves to experience the age-old text as if for the very first time. Moser wrestled with each image until he was satisfied. His goal was to "make the book more accessible in the intimacy of the imagery."

Feeling intimidated when facing a challenge can happen to all of us. Stay focused on your goals – and it may be surprising how fears fall by the wayside.

I love You, O Lord my strength. (Psalm 18:1)

In You, Holy Trinity, I find my strength and courage to succeed.

When Creativity Loses its Spark

Consider what writer Diane Ackerman, author of 17 books, says about creativity: "Writing is my form of celebration and prayer, but it is also the way in which I inquire about the world. I've always imagined worlds and fiddled with words. I frequently find myself in a state of complete rapture about a subject."

What a wonderful way to view writing and creativity! Most of us would like to rediscover the creative spark within us, but the stresses and pressures of everyday life often dampen them.

These suggestions may help reawaken your creative spirit:

Learn the *new* Three R's: Record, Recall and Re-create. Keep a journal. Record an event and you'll recall it.

Nap: some of our most creative insights occur in dreams.

Exercise your brain: practice memorization techniques, visualization and meditation.

Let my prayer be counted as incense...the lifting up of my hands as an evening sacrifice. (Psalm 141:2)

Lord God, renew and inspire my spirit through my relationship with You.

Winner or Loser?

What does failure mean?

It seems how people generally describe failure has evolved over the decades. For example, according to a *New York Times* article, in the early 1800's, to be a failure meant basically one thing: to go bankrupt in business.

Today, the concept of failure is not so cut and dried. Some may believe a person fails if he or she isn't materially successful. Others believe if you're not riding the success of the technology wave, you haven't "made it." Still others regard the term more spiritually, and believe failure means that a person doesn't live up to his or her full potential, or he or she isn't happy or at peace.

It's tempting to judge others, and label someone a failure based on our own interpretation of success. Each of us, however, may have a unique and personal path to success. One person's success could be another's failure. And vice versa.

We beseech You, give us success!
(Psalm 118:25)

Father God, in Jesus' name I pray that the Holy Spirit help me keep You as my focus.

Defining Self-Assurance

According to Webster's dictionary, self-assurance is confidence in one's self, one's powers and one's abilities.

An article in *Self* magazine defined self-assurance more completely. Self-assurance, according to writer Ruth Whitney, says, "I belong here;" "I deserve it;" "I will win." Yet it knows how and why and when to compromise.

She draws a distinction between self-assurance and self-confidence. While self-confidence can be cocky and brash, self-assurance is centered and calm. Nor can self-assurance be eroded the way self-confidence can be eroded.

Who among your family and friends is self-assured? Are you? How can you develop your belief in your self and your powers? Remember, self-assurance is vital to fulfilling your God-given mission in life.

**My Creator chose the place for My tent.
(Sirach 24:8)**

Creator, You loved us into life, gave us Your Son, and even now send Your Spirit to abide with us. May we learn to value ourselves as You do.

Workers, Not Master Builders

When Oscar Romero was named archbishop of San Salvador in 1977, he was known as a good man, but hardly one to rock the political boat. Yet, speaking out for his people against an oppressive government, he became a target. Three years later, he was shot dead at the altar as he celebrated Mass.

Archbishop Romero believed that we are all part of God's plans, that while we cannot do everything, we can do something: "It may be incomplete, but it is a beginning, a step along the way, an opportunity for the Lord's grace to enter and do the rest.

"We may never see the results, but that is the difference between the Master Builder and the worker. We are workers, but not master builders… ministers, not messiahs. We are prophets of a future that is not our own."

Build for the future. Build up God's Kingdom.

Neither the one who plants nor the one who waters is anything, but only God who gives the growth. (1 Corinthians 3:7)

Eternal Lord, show me how to be a faithful worker.

Lessons from a Seven-Year-Old

Katherine Kelly wanted a certain bicycle for her seventh birthday and she knew just Whom to ask. Every night, and again on Sundays at Mass, Katherine and God had some very serious conversations about this perfect bike and its importance to her. She made it plain to Him that it was her one greatest desire.

It was plain to her parents, too, though they knew they couldn't afford it. On her birthday, they presented her with the sturdy, pretty, second-hand bike that they had found room for in the budget. They worried about her disappointment. "I want you to know, Kathy," her father explained, trying to soften the blow, "God can't always answer every prayer."

Katherine looked at him, confused. "But he did answer my prayers, Daddy. He just said 'no'."

As Katherine rode off, smiling, her parents were reminded that faith should never be underestimated.

The Lord is my chosen portion and my cup. (Psalm 16:5)

I know You are with me, Lord. Help me always to be with You.

Ten Precepts or Ten Commandments or...?

Who would ever say that it's a bad thing to teach children good moral values?

In the Indiana town of Scottsburg this became a topic of conversation and controversy as people struggled over the matter of school prayer. Also at issue: the definition of "moral values," who should teach them and where.

Instead of posting the Ten Commandments in violation of the First Amendment, the school board devised the Ten Precepts. These include: trust in God; honor your parents and family; resolve conflicts without violence, avoid being jealous of what others have.

"You've got to try to help steer kids right," said one resident who worries about evil in the world.

Teaching children good moral values begins and ends in the home. But every community and society need to seriously examine principles that affect the well-being of all.

Train children in the right way. (Proverbs 22:6)

Give us a measure of Your wisdom, Father.

Those Surprising Birds

Life is full of surprises. For instance, a great place to go birding is in the midst of a city with over eight million people, plus apartment houses, skyscrapers, factories, cultural and educational institutions and hospitals. The place: New York City.

Birders spot over 200 species in a year. It can become a social event when someone spots a special feathery friend. One long-eared owl regularly draws crowds as it perches near the Metropolitan Museum of Art on Fifth Avenue.

"The long-eared owl is yet another reminder of what birders have long known: Central Park, a green rectangle in a sea of cement smack in the middle of a migratory route, is one of the top birding spots in the country," notes a city newspaper writer.

Some might be surprised that New Yorkers, stereotyped as brusque and impatient, stop to observe the owl and to talk with one another about its beauty. But it's a wise person who remains open to surprise.

Judge with right judgment. (John 7:24)

Open our hearts and minds to the unexpected, Lord.

A Changing Perspective

The weekly bulletin for St. Agnes' Church in New York offered some anonymous thoughts that ring true.

- Funny how a $100 bill looks so big when you take it to church, but so small when you take it to the mall.

- Funny how long a couple of hours spent at church are, but how short they are when watching a movie.

- Funny how we can't think of anything to say when we pray, but we don't have difficulty thinking of things to talk about to a friend.

- Funny how hard it is to read a chapter of the Bible, but how easy it is to read 100 pages of a best selling novel.

- Funny how people want to get a front seat at any game, but scramble to get a back seat at church services.

Give some thought to your own viewpoint. It may not be funny. But it could be very revealing.

I will judge you...according to your ways, says the Lord God. (Ezekiel 18:30)

Holy Spirit, help me see things from Your point of view.

Baked in Goodness

"Bread making takes time and patience and care," wrote Cynthia Hopkins in *Catholic Digest*. "Bread making slows me down. It's as if the comforting aroma emanating from the oven makes everything right." Bread, in fact, is the foundation of many family meals. Bread is also an ancient part of celebration – and religious ritual. Two loaves of challah are blessed in each Jewish home at the Sabbath dinner, in thanks for God's abundance.

"I am the Bread of Life," Jesus told us, and so Catholics and many other Christians celebrate this Eucharist when bread becomes the Body of Christ.

"I like the idea that this humble food, so rich in history, so plentiful in good things, is given as a gift between friends," Hopkins continued, "and that we are nourished by the food and the friendship."

Bread begins then with the good things of the earth–and brings forth good things for relationships and for the soul.

One does not live by bread alone. (Luke 4:4)

Blessed Trinity, enable us to so leaven our world by our deeds that it will be more just and humane.

The Garden of Angels

Three years ago, Debi Faris buried an infant.

She also gave the infant a name, Michael. If she had done nothing, Michael would have been cremated and his remains put in a numbered cardboard box. Michael was an abandoned baby, one of scores left in public places each year in America, and Debi Faris just a woman who heard about him and believed this anonymous baby boy deserved a proper burial.

So began the Garden of Angels. It's where Michael is buried, as well as Nathan, left in a trash bin, Dora, washed up on a beach and dozens more. Why does she do it? "They bring you a child wrapped in plastic and you look in their face."

Ms. Faris has also become an advocate of legislation which offers legal protection to parents who abandon babies in safe places. And it's all because one day she was moved to make a difference for a baby she had never known.

Learn to do good; seek justice. (Isaiah 1:17)

Lord, grant me the wisdom to know my call to action and the strength to follow it through.

Amazing Grace

Known as "The Great Blasphemer," John Newton had a reputation for profanity, coarseness and debauchery. He had even dealt in the slave trade. Yet eventually he was ordained a priest of the Church of England and wrote the hymn, *Amazing Grace.*

In 1748, during an Atlantic storm, his ship almost sank as Newton, lashed to the helm, tried to keep it on course. His thoughts kept turning to Christ though he felt beyond hope. Still, God *might* hear him. He was right. Later, Newton said that the Lord's amazing grace delivered him "that day...out of deep water."

Throughout his life, Newton never ceased to be amazed by God's grace. Before his death he told friends, "I remember two things: that I am a great sinner, and that Christ is a great Savior."

How have you experienced Christ's grace today?

The torrents of perdition assailed me; the cords of Sheol entangled me; the snares of death confronted me. ...He heard my voice...He drew me out of mighty waters. He delivered me. (Psalm 18:4-5,6,16-17)

Thank You for Your amazing and good grace, Father.

Lost and Found

Ever wonder where lost mail and packages end up? Ask Vera Rodriquez Schneider, who has worked at the U.S. Postal Services' Mail Recovery Center in St. Paul, Minnesota, for 13 years.

Her day begins at 7 a.m., in a cramped, stuffy office, opening the boxes, cartons and letters that never reached their destinations. Some of these parcels lack return addresses and are unaddressed; others simply cannot be deciphered. "You have to play detective," Ms. Schneider says.

Why does she find her work so satisfying? It's simple: When she does successfully link a package to its sender or receiver, "people are so happy," she says.

How could your work become more fulfilling? Are you following a path that you believe God intended for you?

Whoever does the will of God is My brother and sister and mother. (Mark 3:35)

Precious Lord, guide me toward the path You want me to walk.

"Bo Knows"

From winning the Heisman Trophy to an all-star career in both football and baseball, Bo Jackson's athletic ability and versatility was unparalleled.

The eighth of ten children in a Bessemer, Alabama, family, Vincent Jackson got his nickname when his brothers shortened the word "boar," as in "wild boar." He cultivated an image as a tough kid because classmates teased him about his stuttering. When his mother threatened him with reform school after he and his friends got into some trouble, Jackson channeled his energy into athletics, winning two state decathlons.

About winning the Heisman, he said, "It's like being in an elite fraternity. I was chosen out of thousands of athletes to get in the club. It's an honor."

Bo Jackson overcame adversity in his younger years, and went on to become a sports great before his career was cut short by injury. He took what he was given and made the most of it.

Keep up your courage. (Acts 27:25)

Lord, may we run to glory thanks to You.

Unconditional Love from a Furry Friend

Caring for a disabled loved one is a very stressful activity that can increase blood pressure and heart rate. Caregivers need to take care of themselves. Some get assistance from four-legged friends.

Karen Allen, Ph.D., assistant professor of medicine at the State University of New York, Buffalo, studied men and women whose spouses had suffered a traumatic brain injury.

Half of the selected caregivers were asked to adopt a dog from a local shelter. All of them wore ambulatory blood pressure monitors. After six months, the pet owners had significantly reduced blood pressure.

Allen credits "the presence of someone who you're really attached to, who...is always on your side." She added that "dogs are great – they're never evaluative, they just love you."

Love, in its many forms, is truly life-giving.

Support the weak. (Acts 20:35)

Jesus, support me in my times of weakness.

A Caring Community

In Racine, Wisconsin, the focus of the work of 8,600 volunteers is the Root River. Volunteers, divers and boaters of all races, ages and economic levels helped to remove nine tons of garbage, 5,700 pounds of metal and 600 tires from the river.

But good deeds were not restricted to the Racine river. Another 130 different projects touched the lives of the hungry, homeless and helpless. For example, instead of bus fare one day, commuters were encouraged to pay in canned goods. 1,000 items were given. In another program, 330 people donated 110 pints of blood. Dentists gave checkups to poor children and landlords reached out to needy seniors with home repairs and reconstruction projects.

It's amazing what happens when people get together for the common good.

Do what is right and good. (Deuteronomy 6:18)

Wherever two or three gather, Lord, I know You are there, filling us with Your compassion and Your strength.

Make a List, Make a Change

Feeling overwhelmed? Take a deep breath, get something to write with and make a list.

Sounds like obvious advice, but it's something that stressed out people often don't do, says F. Washington Jarvis, headmaster of Boston's Roxbury Latin and a devoted maker of lists.

By getting the work out of your mind and onto paper, Jarvis says, you take away the mystery, and make it manageable. He recounts how student after student has come to him under a seemingly hopeless workload, saying there is no time to make a list. But soon the students realize the simple wisdom of the advice.

Writing things out lets you see what you have to do and, maybe even more importantly, what you thought you had to do but really don't – at least not right away.

Prioritize. Check things off when they're done. You'll be surprised at what a list can do.

From your youth choose discipline. (Sirach 6:18)

Guide our decisions, Holy Spirit.

Resting on the Edge

God blessed the seventh day because on it, God rested from all the work that he had done in creation.

This concept has nearly escaped us. We are so geared to productivity that we have almost lost track of Sabbath and sabbatical.

In her series on the Jubilee Year, Sister Paulette Anne Ducharme notes that the people of Leviticus were called to observe the Sabbath not just for one day each week, but for an entire year.

Every 50th year the land was to lie fallow, unplanted. Ducharme interprets this as saying we need time to contemplate without activity. "The secret to our happiness is found within the quiet depths of that solitude," she writes.

Maybe not today, maybe not tomorrow, but there will be a natural break in the flow of your life. Will you be prepared to rest?

Come away...and rest a while. (Mark 6:31)

Take away my fears, Divine Master; let me trust in Your providence during every stage of my life.

High Hopes for Special Kids

Mary Guthrie expects big things from the children in her Giant Step daycare center, and she gets results. Guthrie started the center for kids with special needs. "Many were supposed to be dead if parents would have believed the experts," she says.

Guthrie herself lost one son to sudden infant death syndrome; her daughter, Mickey, who's hearing-impaired, is Giant Step's co-director. Another son, Allen, was born with a seizure disorder and developmental problems. "I created this center," says Guthrie, "as the place I wish I could have taken my son back in 1973." Today Allen drives a car and helps out at the center.

Guthrie, an enthusiastic cuddler, is by no means a coddler. But she's open to any and all children. "We're all the same. We just want to be loved and accepted." She says, "Most people see stone walls. I see a stone wall and start looking how I can pole-vault over."

What do you see?

Hope does not disappoint us. (Romans 5:5)

Help me believe that anything is possible, Mighty God.

Making a Difference

For a decade, *USA Weekend's* has sponsored an annual "Make A Difference Day." Million of people have volunteered to change lives by showing how much they care.

Ed Dixon, a homeless man in Tulsa, Oklahoma, raised $1000 at a concert and helped a shelter that had given him groceries.

In Sparks, Nevada, Diane Vaden, Kristal DeRuise and Kristal's little brother, Trevor, earned $1000 for lupus research by selling their hand painted "ladybug" rocks.

Andrew Libka, a 10-year-old, held a garage sale. He donated $307.73 toward a cancer center in Alpena, Michigan.

Working through Casas por Cristo, Maida Apodaca raised $2500 for materials and recruited 16 workers to build a house in Anapra, Mexico. New homeowner, Paula Luna Garcia, said, "All good things come from the Lord, but you were the means."

Each of us gives to others. The best gift? Our very selves.

To each is given a manifestation of the Spirit for the common good. (1 Corinthians 12:7)

May I emulate Your generosity, Loving Lord.

The Art of Simply "Being."

The Beatles once sang, "Let it be." Today spiritual teacher Isaac Shapiro says that peace and happiness are within reach if we give up doing, seeking and striving – if we, simply are. Shapiro, who grew up in South Africa during apartheid, is a devotee of the Advaita yoga tradition.

"Bring your attention to the living God...in you," advises Shapiro. "Try it for an instant. When the mind goes to this or that thought, bring it home."

In an ever more frenetic world, taking time to simply be is an invaluable activity. Or as Shapiro recommends, "First thing in the morning, take a moment for peace. One moment is enough. Your whole day will be different."

God's peace can transform our lives, if we only let it.

In the morning, while it was still very dark, He got up and went out to a deserted place and there He prayed. (Mark 1:35)

Allow me to find the love and harmony at my core, Spirit of Peace.

Supporting Religious Freedom

Many residents of Flushing, New York, had never heard of the 1657 "Flushing Remonstrance" until the state archives loaned the priceless document to a local library for display. Now many people are coming to appreciate what historians believe to be the first recorded defense of religious freedom in the New World.

"I never heard of it until I saw it here," said library patron Quaiser Malik who is a college student. "I am a Muslim and I love this country because of the laws that protect my religious faith."

The document originated when Quakers were prohibited from worshipping because they weren't members of the Dutch Reformed Church. A group of English freeholders would neither condemn the Quakers nor would they "stretch out (their) hands against them, to punish, banish or persecute them."

Protect freedom of religion remembering that faith in any religion is a free gift.

You were called to freedom. (Galatians 5:13)

Keep us vigilant, Jesus, in protecting precious freedoms.

The Power of Observation

You'd be amazed at what you can learn when you stop, look and wonder.

Professor John Stilgoe, the author of *Outside Lies Magic* and other works, doesn't go past even the most mundane fixtures of rural or urban landscapes without pausing because they offer a window on history. He combines curiosity with a keen sense of observation.

The Harvard University professor, who studies the history of landscape development, believes that manhole covers, fire hydrants, lampposts, mailboxes, old street signs and the like are "portals into the past." He says, "You can learn a great deal about America by taking a look at our backyards."

Being attentive to details whether in your neighborhood, or in a business, personal or spiritual relationship *is* an education. Be more willing to be a student of your world.

Observe carefully what is before you. (Proverbs 23:1)

Holy Spirit, open the eyes of my heart, mind and soul as well as my physical eyes.

The Family That Runs Together

In an event such as the New York City Marathon, there are countless human interest stories.

Andrew Leitch, ran with his father to strengthen their bond. After his mother died, Andrew had a new appreciation of life's ephemeral nature and wanted to "run the marathon with him," said Leitch. "I thought this would be something memorable I could do with my dad." They finished in under five hours.

Justin Rubenstein who had listened for two years to his grandfather and uncle "return home from running the marathon with these wonderful stories," crossed the finish line with "two other generations."

Not every family can run together, but all can share something mutually enjoyable.

There is...a time to laugh...a time to dance... a time to embrace...a time to love. (Ecclesiastes 3:1,4,5,8)

Support the efforts of multi-generational families to enjoy each others' company, God.

Whose Fault Is It?

Want to feel more positive and upbeat when you're caught in traffic? Listen to Craig Boldman and Pete Matthews, authors of *Every Excuse in the Book: 714 Ways to Say "It's Not My Fault!"*

If traffic's creeping be grateful that: When the radio traffic copter describes the jam, you can shout, "That's me!"

You won't get pulled over for speeding.

You're ahead of the person in your rearview mirror.

You can take time to enjoy the potholes.

You might as well spend as much time on the road your taxes paid for as possible.

You don't have to worry about motion sickness.

You can spend quality time with yourself.

Find the humor in every situation. It makes the daily grind a little easier to bear.

Enjoy yourself. (Ecclesiastes 2:1)

Lord, enable me to relax and laugh at life's craziness.

Gratitude: More than 10%

What is gratitude and how can you express it? One writer addresses these questions in her book *Mary Hunt's Debt-Proof Living*.

Hunt believes in tithing, the act of giving the first ten percent of one's income away. For Hunt, this biblically based activity is "a tangible way I can say thank you for everything I have and for every way I have been blessed."

Tithing connects a person to the world by revealing "how vast the need...and how unimportant my stuff is by comparison."

Importantly, it connects one to God, because it acknowledges that "without God's grace and blessing we would have nothing." It is also a way to prove one's trust in God and faith in His care.

Where to give is up to you. Hunt suggests listening to God's direction in your heart.

Bring the full tithe into the storehouse...see if I will not...pour down for you an overflowing blessing. (Malachi 3:10)

Sustaining God, help us trust in Your Providence.

Not Gone and Not Forgotten

Some people think malaria is a disease long since conquered. Yet it continues to infect and kill millions, including at least one child every 30 seconds. And despite scientists' efforts, malaria has recently appeared in drug-resistant strains.

But J. Kevin Baird, PhD, who has contracted the disease seven times in 12 years while doing research, believes it is only a matter of time before a vaccine emerges to stop malaria. The malaria program director at the Naval Medical Research Unit in Jakarta, Baird works with others to develop a vaccine. "It is an incredibly resourceful parasite," he says of the disease spread through mosquito bites.

You, too, have what it takes to make a difference in the lives of others. In ways large or small, every day you can do something positive to help solve problems or ease pain.

As an example of suffering and patience, beloved, take the prophets. ...who showed endurance. (James 5:10-11)

Jesus, teach me to learn from others' trials and sacrifices. In doing so, I honor their efforts and become a better person.

Juggling: Hazardous to Health

Ever see a commuter, cell phone in one hand, cup of coffee in the other and a stressed-out look on his or her face? That tension shows that trying to "do it all" by "multi-tasking," can go too far.

Atlanta businesswoman Sharon Bair often found herself racing through airports, cell phone to her ear, dodging passersby, her eyes glued to the airline departure monitor. When she saw another business traveler so caught up in making his plane (while talking on a cell phone) that he nearly trampled a frail elderly woman, she saw a reflection of her own behavior.

Now, Bair makes it a point to "slow down, open my eyes, ears and heart." Do the same. Practice noticing the sights around you and resting in the present. It's healthier for you and those around you.

Do not worry about tomorrow, for tomorrow will bring worries of its own. Today's trouble is enough for today. (Matthew 6:34)

Help me become a focused, composed person, Lord, so that I may serve others with a clear mind and heart.

Service, Family Style

It costs less than a day at the amusement park – and it's more soul-satisfying. What is it? Service, family style.

Take the Champlins of Leawood, Kansas. Nancy, her husband, Brad, and their three children volunteer regularly. Last Christmas, they adopted a needy family. In the spring, they helped plant a garden and volunteered at a local shelter.

"I wanted us to do things as a family that would afford my children the opportunity to give something back to the community," says Brad. "The service has created a deep bond within our family," Nancy adds.

Says Virginia T. Austin, executive director of Family Matters: "Family volunteering will bring you closer together, help children learn about those in need and encourage adults to model teamwork and…giving."

Serve as you would want to be served.

**Love one another as I have loved you.
(John 15:12)**

Master, You gave Your life for us, so much did You love us. Help me love others with Your love.

A Funny Man with a Serious Message

Garry Marshall is a show business success story. He created and produced such television hits as *Happy Days, Laverne & Shirley* and *The Odd Couple*. He has written plays and acted in films and television.

But for Marshall, family is more important than fame and fortune. "Life is more important than show business. Your personal life has to take precedence over your professional life for you to achieve success in both," he says.

In the 1970s, coming home exhausted, he would often find a book report written by one of his children on the stairs leading to his bedroom. "No matter how tired I was, I always tried to find the energy to read it so it would be ready before school the next morning," he says.

Still, Marshall wants his legacy to be laughter. "There's always so much need for laughter. Somebody has to help lighten the load." Lightening the load is a challenge for us all.

Bear one another's burdens. (Galatians 6:2)

You are the source of all my joy, Master.

Learning While Lending a Hand

The first visit of a group Kentucky teenagers to the "Big Apple" involved volunteering, sightseeing and growing as a group.

The 15 girls and boys from Lexington Catholic High came to New York City to help residents of a poor neighborhood and perhaps to get some valuable lessons to take back home.

The teenagers prepared and served food at a soup kitchen, cleaned rooms at a homeless shelter, and helped set up a summer camp program for children.

"We all grew as a group," said senior Lisa Supko. She and the other students who traveled with her want to let their schoolmates know that "they can make a difference."

Leaving the familiar can be an enriching experience. But it's not necessary to go far to find people who need a helping hand.

Open your hand to the poor. (Deuteronomy 15:11)

Divine Father, inspire us to reach out to those in need.

Honesty – and Good Detective Work

There are many honest people in the world. Some of them are also excellent detectives.

Frank Sweeney discovered a purse on a Manhattan sidewalk. Opening it, he found personal items, photos and credit cards that read "Venus Williams," the same name as the tennis great. But, after all, how likely was that, he thought?

Heading home to try contacting the owner, Sweeney noticed a number of limos outside a hotel. They bore signs announcing a sportsperson of the year award. Wondering if his initial assumption about the purse owner's identity might be right, the "detective" questioned a driver. Athletes attending the event were indeed staying at the hotel.

Sweeney spoke with the hotel's security chief. Within minutes, the honest detective was being hugged by a grateful young woman, tennis star Venus Williams.

Value honesty and creative, critical thinking, as well.

Honesty comes home to those who practice it. (Sirach 27:9)

Spirit of Wisdom, show me how to use my talents for the good of my brothers and sisters.

Shaking Life for All It's Worth

When architect Ed Towbin was in his 50s, a job seminar made him see that he'd had it with satisfying clients' needs.

He considered early retirement. Despite being an avid weekend painter, he wasn't sure he wanted to devote all his time to art. Then Towbin talked to his boss. They agreed to cut back his work schedule so he would have two days a week to paint.

Three years later, Towbin left his job. Another three years and the former architect had a successful one-man show, and even a favorable write-up in an art review.

"People who challenge themselves regularly score significantly higher on life-satisfaction tests," says Elizabeth Somer, author of *Age-Proof Your Body: Your Complete Guide to Lifelong Vitality.* "Vibrant people in their 70s, 80s and 90s tell me the key is to 'shake life for all it's worth.'"

A joyful heart is life itself and rejoicing lengthens one's life. (Sirach 30:22)

Master, help me to always use wisely the gifts and talents You gave me.

Highly Sensitive People

Are you sensitive to loud noises? Do big crowds drive you crazy? Do you cover your ears when fire trucks roar past?

If you answered yes to these questions, you may be what psychologist Elaine Aron calls a "highly sensitive person," or HSP. These are physically or genetically sensitive individuals who are highly attuned to the world around them. "The senses are heightened," she says.

What are the traits of an HSP? In her book, *The Highly Sensitive Person in Love*, Aron says the key is "sensitivity to subtleties. HSP's brains process information more deeply. They are easily overwhelmed and need more quiet time. A less sensitive person, on the other hand, does not notice as much. They handle the stress of daily living better and don't need as much quiet time.

Your temperament is God's gift to you. Use it for good.

(You) formed my inward parts; You knit me together in my mother's womb. I praise You, for I am fearfully and wonderfully made. (Psalm 139:13-14)

Father, help me appreciate others' feelings as well as my own.

In His Father's Image

The late baseball Hall of Famer, Roberto Clemente, once said, "Anytime you have the opportunity to make things better and you don't, then you are wasting your time."

Clemente never hesitated to help a child, a neighbor, a friend, even those he didn't know. He died when his plane crashed on the way to bring relief to Nicaragua after an earthquake in 1973.

His son, Roberto, Jr. was only six at the time but remembers that his father "was always there for people who needed him. He never turned anyone away."

Now he's taken his father's example to heart. Clemente Jr., a sportscaster, helps the Latino community through the Roberto Clemente Foundation as well as other foundations and sports programs.

It's important to both give and receive good example daily.

I have set you an example, that you also should do as I have done to you. (John 13:15)

Enable us to live by Your example, Jesus of Nazareth.

Lessons about Teamwork

How would you define success?

The basketball teams of DeMatha Catholic High School in Hyattsville, Maryland, have achieved stunning success over the years. They have won at least 20 games 43 straight seasons, 31 conference titles and five national championships, with Morgan Wootten at the helm.

Wootten, the winningest coach in basketball history, emphasizes education and selflessness; requires attention to detail; a team-first attitude; the priority of religion, family and schoolwork over basketball.

He uses poems (Kipling's *If* is a favorite) and lessons to mold the players. A player says, "It's about growing spiritually as well as on the court" so that they emerge as well-rounded individuals.

Wootten says success means "these kids go on and continue their education, grow in life and become useful citizens."

That's a great definition.

Be strong and very courageous...act in accordance with all the Law...that you may be successful. (Joshua 1:7)

Help me remember that there is no "I" in "team", Father.

Save Now!

If you're like most people, you're probably not saving enough money for the future. The cost of living has skyrocketed and many struggle just to pay the bills.

But procrastination with saving leads to "surviving instead of thriving". Dan Benson, a financial advisor and writer, recommends a ruthless steering of money into a savings account.

How? Make it a priority. Benson cites a story by George S. Clason called *The Richest Man In Babylon*. Everyone wonders how Arkad, the main character, accumulated his wealth. His secret formula: "A part of all I earn is mine to keep."

Strive for financial independence by making savings a priority. Learn about automatic saving plans. Plan your donations or tithing. Pay yourself as well as your bills.

It's not easy to save, but it's well worth the effort.

Give me the Wisdom that sits by Your throne ...she will guide me wisely in my actions. (Wisdom of Solomon 9:4, 11)

Remind me to ask only for what I need, Provider.

Lifetime Career: Eliminating Injustice

On the very first "Take Our Daughters to Work Day" in 1993, Nell Merlino was perhaps the most nervous person in the country. You see the communications consultant was responsible for coordinating the event with women's groups everywhere.

When Merlino turned on the television early that morning, she saw a little girl announcing the weather. Suddenly aware of the impact of her efforts, "I was sitting by myself, sobbing."

Merlino continually turns down offers for high-paying consulting positions with large firms. Instead, she focuses her time, talent and energy on a single mission: changing the way society views and treats women. She is now working on an economic development project.

Working to end injustice may seem an impossible task. Yet, one person can make a difference. How can you use your talents to promote justice?

A person is justified by works and not by faith alone. (James 2:24)

Jesus, help us follow Your lead, and treat people without discrimination or prejudice.

A Class Act

Ann Connolly Tolkoff asked her high school class to memorize and deliver a portion of Lincoln's Gettysburg Address. One teen, from Vietnam, rose to the lectern and began, "Four-score and seven years ago..." but was interrupted by a late student, who taunted the speaker. Tolkoff made the troublemaker leave class. The student finished the Address with such enthusiasm that he moved Tolkoff to tears.

When the principal let the troublemaker return, Tolkoff was angry. Later she shared her frustration with fellow teacher, Sarah Kass, and the two decided to start their own school.

"City on a Hill" opened as the first public charter high school in Massachusetts founded, designed and run by teachers. Its mission: "To graduate responsible, resourceful and respectful democratic citizens." Although facing academic challenges, the school boasts a 90 percent attendance rate and a large number of graduates who go on to college.

In important matters, keep your expectations high.

Train children in the right way. (Proverbs 22:6)

Father, help me touch someone with Your love.

Remembering a Friend

They were only six at the time, but best buddies. All David Glattstein wanted to do was cheer up his sick friend, Matthew Kamin, so David planned to give Matthew his own favorite stuffed animal. But when David and his parents arrived at the hospital, they were told that Matthew, who had had leukemia, had died.

David found a way to honor him 12 years later. Using his own money, he established a scholarship for a student from Swampscott (Massachusetts) High School in his friend's name.

The first recipient of the $1000 award was Liana Bryanos. David Glattstein recognized a winner the minute he read her essay on how to make the most of life. It, he says, had "the heart and passion for people that Matthew Kamin had in life."

What a wonderful way to honor a dead friend. May we all revere and hold close our dearest relationships.

Faithful friends are a sturdy shelter...a treasure ...beyond price...life-saving medicine. (Sirach 6:14,15, 16)

Help me treasure the gift of friendship, Christ.

Secrets to Simplifying

Just too much stuff? Overwhelming clutter? Create space in your life, in your mind, in your heart: simplify. The more you possess, the more overcrowded your life becomes.

Clean out your closet. Pass unworn shoes and clothing to a secondhand store. In the bathroom get rid of unnecessary and unused possessions. Limit shopping.

Successfully decluttering? Make time for family and friends. Chronically overbooked? List the things of greatest importance and you'll see where you can cut unnecessary obligations. Build pauses into each day. Take a look at the stress-promoters in your life and tame them.

Simplifying is not easy, but the rewards are great. One of them: spending time with God brings spiritual peace.

Choose life. (Deuteronomy 30:19)

Father, help me to determine my priorities, to realize that less can be more and more can be less.

A Star Plays a Supporting Role

Latinos may be the most underrepresented ethnic group in the arts world. Jimmy Smits, the Hispanic star of television's *L.A. Law* and *NYPD Blue*, wanted to help change that.

He and his various co-stars had worked on voting drives but he never felt it was enough. "Was it just a photo opportunity...or did we actually do something?" the Emmy and Golden Globe award winner wondered.

So in 1997, Smits co-founded the National Hispanic Foundation for the Arts (NHFA) to help the entertainment industry "reflect society." They award scholarships to financially needy Hispanic students at eight premier graduate programs. Smits says, "College was the springboard for my success, and I wanted to support that." The NHFA also arranges internships and supports a network of professionals.

Supporting young people builds a better future for all.

On a day of salvation I have helped you. (Isaiah 49:8)

With your help, I will put my all into my efforts, Jesus.

Getting in Shape for a New Job

Corporate executives may have demanding careers and preparing for them can be stressful. But there are some jobs where you literally have to get into shape for the interview.

Want to be a lifeguard in Los Angeles County? Forget it if you can't complete a 1,000-meter ocean swim. If you make the cut, you'll face eight days of challenges including ten kilometer soft-sand runs and a 1,000-meter run-swim-run-swim-runs.

For aspiring employees of the New York City Sanitation Department, there are physical tests to demonstrate such skills as the ability to drag and lift baskets loaded with weighted bags.

F.B.I. agents need to be able to run as well as do pull-ups, push-ups and sit-ups. The Secret Service likely has its own fitness requirements, though they're not talking.

Think twice if your office job seems boring. Bringing interest and energy to your tasks can make everything worthwhile.

Be content with what you have. (Heb. 13:5)

Help us to appreciate what we have, Lord.

You Do a Lot More

There's a story that bears out the phrase "you never know."

Mark was walking home from high school when a boy ahead of him dropped his books and a bunch of other things. Mark helped him pick them up. Since they were headed the same way they started talking and wound up spending the afternoon together.

Over the next few years Mark and the other boy, Bill, became friends. As graduation neared, Bill asked, "Did you ever wonder why I was carrying so much stuff home that day? I cleaned out my locker because I didn't want to leave a mess... I was going home to commit suicide. But after we had such a good time, I realized I would have missed many other good times... When you picked up my books that day... You saved my life."

Behind each face we meet are the complexities of being human. And kindness is always the best greeting we can offer.

I have set you an example, that you also should do as I have done to you. (John 13:15)

Loving Lord, may my countenance always reflect Yours.

Cooperation: It Works!

It is unfortunate that archaeologists and Native Americans have historically worked at cross-purposes, with tensions running high between the two groups for years. Archaeologists seek relics, information and access to land and sites that potentially hold answers to ancient mysteries. Native Americans reject tampering with what they consider sacred land, objects and human remains.

Yet controversy doesn't have to be the norm, say Jeffrey Hantman, Karenne Wood and Dianne Shields. They are working together to study the native people of Virginia.

Karenne Wood is director of historic research for the Monacan Indian Nation. She says that tribal members viewing reconstructions of their ancestors at the Monacan Ancestral Museum in Amherst, Virginia felt "a renewed sense of pride in their Indian heritage."

Cooperation means a willingness to join our goals with those of others to find a solution and, ultimately, success.

**Love one another as I have loved you.
(John 15:12)**

Holy Spirit, bless us with a cooperative spirit so that we may hear others' perspectives and have our own enriched.

The Healing Power of Pets

Tyler, a black Labrador, and Toby, a golden retriever, regularly visit patients in Cincinnati's Children's Hospital Medical Center. They are part of a pet therapy program which seems to help children by boosting their spirits, aiding their recovery, and soothing the fearful.

In order to qualify for the program, dogs must show they are calm and tolerant. Although they can't be ill, they don't have to be in perfect health. "We have a dog who is a chemotherapy survivor", said Dr. Edith Markoff, a founder of the Dog Visitation program. "This is wonderful for our children struggling with cancer and their own treatments."

Another "dog who has a metal plate in his leg and walks with a limp" shows patients in rehabilitation that disabilities don't keep one "from doing good things or being helpful."

Don't let anything stop you from doing good.

The wolf shall live with the lamb, the leopard...with the kid...and a little child shall lead them. (Isaiah 11:6)

Creator, bless the animals that share our lives.

Teaching: a Rewarding Second Career

Teaching is a challenging vocation and it's not for everyone. But if you have what it takes, there are many youngsters who'll take what you have to offer.

Age or a prior profession need not be barriers. More and more older adults are leaving their jobs to enroll in post-college teaching programs. Universities are establishing alternative teacher-certification programs to meet the need.

Chris Cecil was a commodities trader earning six-figures. He traded it in to become a science teacher. His income is less but so is his stress. "Most of all," he says, "I'm having a good time."

Arthur Moore retired after 21 years in the Army and became a teacher. Watching children learn gives him energy. And as an African-American male he finds that "the students look at me as a role model. I'm a father figure as well as a teacher."

Be a teacher in whatever way you can.

Wisdom teaches her children. (Sirach 4:11)

Give us wise and intelligent teachers, God.

A Mixed Picture

Vikings, those brutes of yore, may have gotten some bad press. It seems that, like the rest of us, they were not all good or all evil.

That's not to say that Vikings didn't raid, pillage and terrorize as they explored Europe and beyond. It's just that they did other things as well.

"In fact, the Vikings were a blessing," believes William Fitzhugh, director of the Art Studies Center at the Smithsonian National Museum of Natural History.

According to Fitzhugh, through their exchanges of literature, poetry and art "the Vikings ...actually changed Europe for the better, infusing it with new ideas, initiating contact between different cultures."

In characterizing others, it often pays to keep an open mind.

Do not judge by appearances. (John 7:24)

Teach us tolerance, Savior.

An Ageless Question

Peter F. Drucker, expert in the science of management, has had a question on his mind since he was 13 years old.

"I had an inspiring teacher who once went through the class asking everyone, 'What do you want to be remembered for?' explains Drucker. "None of us, of course, could give an answer."

Drucker recalls his teacher chuckling and saying, "I didn't expect you to be able to respond. But if you still can't by the time you're 50, you will have wasted your life."

Today, Drucker still asks himself the question, "What do I want to be remembered for?" He says, "It induces you to renew yourself because it pushes you to see yourself as the person you can become."

Sometimes looking at what will be said after you've gone will help what you say and do right here and now.

Bless the God of all who...fosters our growth from birth, and deals with us according to His mercy. (Sirach 50:22)

To all things, Creator, You bring order. It is in You that we find our real purpose.

What a Difference 36,500+ Days Make

What if we flipped back the calendar, say, 100 years? What was life like then? Well, it certainly was different. Consider that in the United States:

- only fourteen percent of homes had a bathtub.
- the maximum speed limit in most cities was 10 miles per hour.
- most women washed their hair once a month with borax or egg yolks for shampoo.
- plutonium, insulin and antibiotics hadn't been discovered; scotch tape, crossword puzzles, canned beer and iced tea did not exist.
- one in ten adults couldn't read or write;
- only six percent of Americans had graduated from high school.

Change happens. Time does march on.

Every matter has its time. (Ecclesiastes 8:6)

At all times, Your love for us, Father, knows no limits.

Everyday Spirituality

If you're seeking to enhance your spiritual life, consider these ten suggestions from writer Salley Shannon:

1. Say a prayer when you hear an emergency siren.

2. Memorize some of the Psalms.

3. Plan to be kind to others.

4. Share the human condition by taking at least five minutes every day for a conversation you don't need to have, with for instance, a grocery checker.

5. Pray for others.

6. Tell a troubled friend how faith sustains you.

7. Join and participate in a faith community.

8. Learn about other religious traditions.

10. Make amends.

Small steps can take us far, if we just make the effort.

Be rich in good works. (1 Timothy 6:18)

Lord, show us Your way.

Not So Hot Wheels?

Visit virtually any playground, parking lot, mall or just about anywhere young teens congregate and you'll see them: those metal, kick-powered scooters that are all the rage these days.

Actually, this scooter craze began in Japan a few years ago. It then migrated to Australia, then to the U.S. in 1998. They have saturated the marketplace and kids' wish lists. One toy industry executive predicts that eventually "You'll find them at a yard sale for ten bucks or less."

Fads can be seductive. Often, they promise fun and fulfillment, but more often than not, they turn out to be nothing to shout about.

Learn to value what truly matters.

Strive first for the kingdom of God and His righteousness. (Matthew 6:33)

Help me treasure what is important, what lasts for eternity, Holy God.

The Incredible, Invincible Kudzu

Up close, it's a lovely, lush, emerald-green plant that grows wildly in the American South. Despite its beauty, however, some refer to it as a "dangerous weed that grows like the devil."

It seems kudzu is a highly adaptive, aggressive weed that will grow in either moist or dry conditions, and with little or excessive sunlight. Its vines reach high and wide, overlapping and covering buildings, billboards, or anything else that is stationary.

"You think you've killed it, but it just keeps coming back," says one landscape engineer who works to eradicate kudzu.

But North Carolinian Edith Edwards, among others, sees kudzu differently. She loves to serve fried kudzu leaves, and claims that eating the weed keeps her young.

Kudzu is one of those things that supports the adage, "one person's meat is another's poison."

In everything do to others as you would have them do to you. (Matthew 7:12)

Jesus, help me see the potential and the good in all situations.

How Not to Be a Mom-In-Law

In a playful article by Linda Greider, she offers ideas on how to be a good mother-in-law by giving tongue-in-cheek advice.

"Tell everybody at the wedding that you disapprove of your child's spouse," she advises. "Whenever your daughter-in-law answers the phone, go directly to, "Can I speak to my baby, please?" and "Be sneaky and try to get away with it.""

She came up with these and other tidbits after a conversation with her own two children and their spouses. The bottom line from all four of her advisors? "Don't be a buttinsky."

That's good advice for anyone who has a friend or family member making a life-changing transition. Unconditional love and true friendship mean that if you have concerns, you share them privately and then respect others' choices and commitments. Keep your heart and your door open. You may be lucky enough to watch someone blossom.

Those who love God must love their brothers and sisters also. (1 John 4:21)

God, let me channel Your love to those I care about as they choose new directions in life.

Celebrating Differences

Each one has a little different history. They can be grouped in families and talk to one another or praise the gods. Their sounds can be unique.

An exhibit of drums at the Smithsonian called "Ritmos de Identidad" (Rhythms of Identity) featured handmade drums from the collection of Dr. and Mrs. Joseph H. Howard. Many uniquely carved and decorated instruments from Africa, the United States and the Caribbean were displayed.

"My father felt it was rhythm that was universal," said the Howard's daughter Victoria. Her father showed his children the drum collection as they were growing up and said: "You are the fruit of the cross of cultures, and of the pride they bear. You are children of the world's culture; you are from everywhere, like the drums." Howard's lineage is a mix of African-American, Latino, East Indian, European and Native American.

Research your family's history. Be proud of it.

Ascribe to the Lord, O families of the peoples ...glory and strength. (Psalm 96:7)

Remind me to rejoice in my family, Holy Family.

I Am, I Am, I Am

Carolyn Scott Kortge observes that even Thoreau, who retreated from his routine for a year of living "deliberately," knew the perils of distraction.

She quotes a piece he wrote for the *Atlantic Monthly* in which he said, "I am alarmed when it happens that I have walked a mile into the woods bodily, without getting there in spirit."

How easy it is to live, removed from the present. We arrive at work, unsure of which route we've just driven. Parents find themselves kissing little ones goodnight, realizing they never truly connected with their children that day. Even good friends may discover it has been a long while since they have truly listened to each other.

Kortge has found focus in meditation while walking. She makes a real effort to live in – and focus on – the present. How will you experience today – and tomorrow?

Pay attention. (Mark 4:24)

Thank you for this very moment, Eternal God.

A Prescription for Reading

A 51-year-old high school teacher entered the hospital after a heart attack. Surrounded by tubes, wires and machines, the patient remarked that he felt as if he were "in Peter Coffin's inn."

The teacher was alluding to the proprietor of Spouter-Inn, the lodging house so well known to Ishmael, Queequeg and the other characters in Herman Melville's 1851 novel, *Moby Dick*. The nurse, hearing the word "coffin" and thinking the patient suicidal, called for a psychiatric consult.

It seemed no one at the hospital had read the famous Melville novel.

The lesson, concluded the *New England Journal of Medicine,* which carried a story on the incident, was two-fold. First, medical personnel need to listen more closely to patients' remarks and ask about unfamiliar phrases. Second, doctors and nurses should have a broader education in the humanities.

After all, didn't someone say, "Physician heal thyself"?

(The) gift of healing comes from the Most High. (Sirach 38:2)

Heal me, Lord, and give me strength.

Shortstop Scores A Home Run

When Yankee shortstop Derek Jeter was growing up in Kalamazoo, Michigan, he was a big fan of former Bronx Bomber Dave Winfield. It wasn't only the way he played ball, Jeter admired, but the fact that he had created a foundation to promote health, literacy and self-esteem.

Jeter told his family, "When I make it, that's what I'm going to do." Jeter was as good as his word. Even before he was named Rookie of the Year in 1996, Jeter planned his Turn 2 Foundation, committed to keeping young people away from drugs and alcohol. Jeter's dad Charles, a counselor with a Ph.D. in sociology, now oversees the foundation. Together, they have raised and distributed $1.5 million to substance abuse prevention programs and also established college scholarships.

Jeter is thrilled. "You dream as a youngster to play professional sports," Jeter commented. "I don't think you realize the impact you can have on someone's life."

Make the most of your impact on others.

Remember your leaders. (Hebrews 13:7)

Thank you, King of Kings, for strong young men and women willing to provide leadership for future generations.

A Special Streak

Believe it or not, a suburban Long Island, New York, high school has earned a place in the *Guinness Book of World Records*.

Actually, Miller Place High School now has the longest streak in scholastic sports history. The badminton team has never lost. Ever. Most of the credit has to go to retired coach Patricia McCarrick, once the best 35-and-over national player. She began a varsity team in 1972 and created a club to attract and coach kids. She also started a *phys. ed.* badminton program, beginning with seventh-graders.

But her lasting legacy is the Miller Place Badminton Club Inc., a non-profit organization with world-class coaches and varsity players to teach the game to children as young as second-grade.

In addition, members of the varsity volunteer for a wide range of projects: a quilt for a baby with AIDS; a beach cleanup; teaching kids about fire safety.

Learning about a sport and helping others is a winning situation for everyone.

Live in harmony with one another. (Romans 15:5)

Help me reach out to others, Great Teacher.

An Unusual Omission: Religion

What do the economy, weather, crime, terrorism, sports, drugs and alcohol and education all have in common? When it comes to TV news coverage they receive more airtime in a single week than religion.

Yet many news stories have a serious religious or moral angle to them. "It's infuriating," admits Peggy Wehmeyer, network TV's only full-time religion reporter. Wehmeyer is often questioned by colleagues about her "motives for covering religion." She in turn is often amazed by "the level of ignorance in most newsrooms about the effect of religion in people's lives."

Consider writing to television network programmers, cable stations and local representatives to express your views about this and other media issues that concern you. Change can only happen as a result of action.

If any...do not bridle their tongues...their religion is worthless. Religion...is this: to care for orphans and widows...and to keep oneself unstained by the world. (James 1:27)

God, strengthen and encourage me to work for change.

Being Frank

In his 60s, his face wrinkled with many lines, Frank had spent a lot of time smiling.

A retired widower, he delivered the community newspaper three times a week to offices. Each time, he would wait until the supervisor had finished a telephone call or conversation, and then he would say hello. He loved his work, he would always say, and he loved Jesus too. He also wanted people to know they were beautiful and special.

After Frank's visit, everyone seemed to smile a little more. "It's amazing," said one worker, "how someone can just smile at you on the street and suddenly your whole day feels different. It's such a little thing."

One smile – one word, one act – can indeed change someone's world. The gift of encouragement calls out the finest in the other even if it involves risks, repeated effort and courage. Ask Frank.

Encourage one another. (1 Thessalonians 5:11)

I look to You, Lord, in times of joy and distress. You are my hope always.

The Girl Who Says "Can"

Brooke Ellison graduated from Harvard University with an A-average. Here's one more detail: Brooke is a quadriplegic.

Hit by a car in the seventh grade, she was left paralyzed from the neck down and dependent on a ventilator. She can't walk, breath or drink on her own. But with the help of her mother, Jean, who has been Brooke's constant companion – Jean calls herself the "brawn" to her child's "brains" – Brooke has lived a life of scholarship, friendship and service to others.

She believes in, "continuing to live and not letting what I can't do define what I can." A friend explains that she was chosen to address her graduation class because, "Brooke is living a life that is out there, instead of closing up and looking inward." She and her mother, and indeed the whole family, are extraordinary in their ability to pursue the positive no matter what.

It's a trait worth imitating.

Do not be overcome by evil, but overcome evil with good. (Romans 12:21)

Spirit of Hope, grant me grace to feel gratitude and the wisdom to perceive obstacles as opportunities.

Befriending Yourself

Who is it that puts you down almost every day, but whom you still keep in your life? Who finds it hardest to forgive your failures, but you still have lunch with everyday? Face the mirror, it's you. We are our own toughest critics and least forgiving judges. Surely this is not what God intends for us.

Try keeping a simple list of the negative things you tell yourself during the course of one day. You'll soon see patterns. Spotting them is a chance to eliminate them.

Assign specific times during the day when you will and will not worry about things. You'll benefit from the perspective you gain and your body and soul will appreciate it.

Remember that you are unique, with gifts no other living thing was given. Be as good to yourself as your Creator wants you to be.

'To love (God) with all the heart...understanding, and...strength,' and 'to love one's neighbor as oneself,' – this is much more important than all...offerings and sacrifices. (Mark 12:33)

If we are to appreciate Your creations, Lord, remind us to appreciate ourselves.

What Can One Person Do?

Individuals can become catalysts for change. Baltimore city officials began the Adopt-A-Lot program. Residents were allowed to lease certain vacant city lots at no charge as long as they kept the properties weed and debris free.

Activist Gloria Luster, who runs the Power of Hope Garden, took it a step further when she and Rev. Choyce Hall of St. John's Evangelical Lutheran Church began using a lot to grow fresh produce. They recruited people to prepare the soil, plant the seeds and harvest their crops. Organically grown peppers, tomatoes, beans, cucumbers and other produce provide food for families as well as area soup kitchens.

Influenced by the garden's beauty, residents began a block association to renovate abandoned housing. A plan to start compost piles with kitchen leftovers and construction of a low-cost green-house for year-round gardening were also planned.

What ideas for change do you have?

Good works are conspicuous; and even when they are not, they cannot remain hidden. (1 Timothy 5:25)

Jesus, help me believe I can make a difference.

For the Time Being

Dan Morris, writing in *Catholic New York*, describes a valuable lesson he learned from an oft-repeated phrase of his grandfather's.

It seems Grandpa Morris would often punctuate his projects – fixing up a fishing pole or planning a family camping trip – with, "For the time being." It is a phrase Mr. Morris has now come to understand and appreciate.

He writes, "Things did not have to be perfect for Grandpa to make things happen. Dreams did not become hot-air balloons that would carry him away from what could be done. Done well."

"For the time being" is based on human reality. Much as we'd like to, we can't do all things perfectly all the time. It matters that we try. After all, our imperfect efforts keep the world going 'round. As Mr. Morris notes, "The constant seems to be those folks who consistently see simple human need and simply respond – for the time being."

I have seen a limit to all perfection, but Your commandment is exceedingly broad. (Psalm 119:96)

Holy Spirit, remind me that my efforts matter, I matter, all Your people matter.

No Length Not Worth Going To

Sarah Moody would not bear to watch her grandson suffer from his skin ailment. Unable to sweat, heat could – literally – have killed him. At first she cried, yelled at walls and at God, and eventually, decided that if He wasn't going to solve the problem, she would with His guidance.

Ms. Moody prayed and remained open to every hope of help. One day she had the idea to contact NASA. "If they can keep astronauts cool in space, they must have something for my grandson," she reasoned.

They did. Today, not only does her grandson enjoy the benefits of NASA's technology via the portable cooling system he wears, so do almost seven hundred other children. Sarah Moody spearheaded a campaign to make NASA's technology available to others with similar diseases.

God always helps us, but He also wants us to cooperate.

Be patient in suffering, persevere in prayer. Contribute to the needs of the saints. (Romans 12:12)

Show me, Lord, that I can do Your work at all times and in all places.

Tomorrow's Leaders

Here are some of the points in an e-mail that has been circulating about the latest college graduates.

- They've never seen a television without a remote control.
- Vinyl records are a myth to them.
- "The War" refers to the Persian Gulf crisis.
- Rotary dial telephones – huh?

These observations make us chuckle, but they neglect other characteristics of today's young adults.

- They are the most ethnically diverse graduating class in history.
- More than ever before are going to college.
- They are more tolerant than any previous class.

Our future is in the hands of today's "kids." They *are* up to the challenge. Be trusting. Be a model.

**Leave to the young a noble example.
(2 Maccabees 6:28)**

Keep my heart open to all the blessings of the world, Jesus Christ.

Capturing Spirit, Life on Film

When art and photography aficionados hear the name Austin Hansen, they often think of a singular subject: Harlem. That's because, Hansen, a American photographer popular in the 1930's, possessed the unique ability to capture the social, political and domestic spirit of the celebrated New York neighborhood that has been frequently studied, yet often, misunderstood.

Often called a photojournalist, Hansen could translate a person's or place's enthusiasm to film. And, as in his famous portrait of a very young Sugar Ray Robinson, a person's grace and concentration, too. His work is regarded as an expression of a Harlem and its citizens of a bygone era.

Each of us possesses a set of skills and talents that are uniquely ours. How do you express your God-given talents so others' lives may be enriched?

To each is given the manifestation of the Spirit for the common good. (1 Corinthians 12:7)

Remind me, Father God, that my talents are a gift from You, and are not to be wasted, ignored or denigrated.

Freedom's Cost

When 19th century poet Ralph Waldo Emerson penned the words, "By the rude bridge that arched the flood,/Their flag to April's breeze unfurled…" he was employing artistic license to rhyme with "The shot heard round the world."

Imagine his surprise when at the centennial of the Concord battle Emerson learned that Nathaniel Page, a minuteman from Bedford, Massachusetts, had actually carried the "Bedford Flag" into battle.

The flag, a thick square of red silk damask on which was painted an armed hand brandishing a sword surrounded by the motto, *Vince Aut Morire* – "Conquer or Die," had remained in the Page family until 1885 when it was given to the local library.

Millions have died to preserve the rights and freedoms symbolized first by the "Bedford Flag" and now by "the Stars and Stripes." Take a few moments to think about the many men and women who gave themselves for a better future, for a better today.

Proclaim liberty throughout the land to all its inhabitants. (Leviticus 25:10)

Lord, bless our nation.

The Art of Negotiation

Marriage and family therapist Marc Snowman, offers these insights on five major obstacles to successful negotiating.

Denial. Rather than admit our anger, we try to rationalize or ignore it hoping it will go away. Instead, accept that something is bothering you.

Trivializing. Sometimes we undercut our partner's feelings by saying "You're too sensitive," or "That's ridiculous." Respect your partner's feelings.

Escalation. Arguments over minor issues can get worse. Stop. Walk away. Cool off. Determine what's angering you.

Globalizing. Statements that begin "You always" and "You never" are unfair and exacerbate situations. Explain what upset you. Offer a compromise.

Relationships are hard work, but can be made easier if we are honest and respectful. It's worth the effort.

Honesty comes home to those who practice it. (Sirach 27:9)

Open our minds and hearts to fairness, Holy Trinity, One God.

Taking On the Media With Children in Mind

When her six-year old son played a violent video game, and a friend shouted "Kill him! Kill him!" because he wasn't killing fast enough, Daphne White realized she had to take action.

Because the Kensington, Maryland woman is convinced that violent entertainment has a negative impact on children, she began the Lion & Lamb Project to "stop the merchandising of violence" to children.

"Kids are getting a very mixed up message about...violence," says White. "If we want to have a less violent future, we have to start with children."

White conducts workshops for parents and has testified before the U. S. Senate. She wants to make today's children, who are very environmentally conscious, just as aware of peace.

World peace can be achieved one person at a time. No cause is too big for a determined individual to do his or her share.

Blessed are the peacemakers, for they will be called children of God. (Matthew 5:9)

Abba, remind me that I am a unique and valued individual who can make a change for the better.

Remembering Harsh Realities

Today, it's hauntingly desolate, the winds blowing past its stone sentry posts across the California desert. But, in 1943, Manzanar Concentration Camp's tarpaper barracks housed 10,000 men, women and children who were of Japanese ancestry.

After the Japanese attack on Pearl Harbor, these mostly American citizens had been arrested, their homes and businesses confiscated under Federal order 9066. Ten concentration camps from California to Arkansas held about 120,000 Japanese-Americans for more than three years

Today, the National Park Service is developing Manzanar as a National Historic Site. "It's important that Americans remember what happened," says retired teacher Kunitomi Embrey. She was 18 when she and her family were sent there. She heads a survivors committee that shares experiences.

Genuine patriotism requires that we work to safeguard the fragile right of equality under the law for every person.

Bring good news to the oppressed...proclaim liberty to the captives, and release to the prisoners. (Isaiah 61:1)

Father, what can I do to help my nation be of all people, by all people and for all people?

Writing: a Powerful Force

Writing. Various civilizations have created their own forms. All are "a system of human communication by means of conventional visible marks linked to spoken language." That includes everything from Mesopotamian Cuneiform (3200 B.C. to A.D. 75) to Egyptian Hieroglyphs (c. 3200 B.C. to A.D. 394) to the various forms of electronic writing being developed.

Writing is a powerful force used throughout time to record and share everything from the frivolous and boring to the poignant and profound. Since it was invented, people have used writing to transmit information and feelings, fight loneliness and even develop a greater a sense of self.

Writing. It's easy to see why writing, learning to write, is so important.

Perhaps there is a letter you should be writing today

See what large letters I make when I am writing in my own hand! (Galatians 6:11)

Jesus, bless the efforts of those overcoming illiteracy.

Get Involved

Here are more ideas on ways to change your corner of the world for the better from Danny Seo's *Heaven on Earth:*

1. Donate used luggage to a foster family agency so that children will not have to use trash bags for their belongings.
2. In the summer months, donate to a food pantry to help ease the burden on families when children aren't eating at school.
3. In the Fall, offer to plant spring flower bulbs at public buildings to help brighten up your community.
4. Pay double your PTA dues and ask that the money be used to pay the fee of a low income parent.
5. Help raise money to build a playground by creating a "sponsor a brick" program. Sponsors buy a brick with their name on it for a predetermined amount.

What other ideas do you have?

The measure you give will be the measure you get. (Matthew 7:2)

Holy Spirit, encourage our efforts to help others.

Sharing Family Stories

Although finding time to share family stories is a challenge, it can be fun to do. In *Catholic Digest*, Debra Ahrens suggests a few ways to pass on your heritage of family stories:

1. Use car time to say: "Oh, I was thinking about the time when…"
2. Talk at the dinner table.
3. Invite everyone to contribute pictures or memorabilia to a family storybook.
4. Use existing family papers and mementoes to trigger memories.
5. Connect to your past in recipes and songs.

Another tip: turn off the TV. Some social commentators believe television has usurped the family's role in transmitting values to the youngest generation.

God formed families because it is not good for us to be alone. Thank God for the families to which you belong.

Ascribe to the Lord, O families…the glory due His Name. (1 Chronicles 16:28,29)

Jesus, inspire us to find new ways to share with our families.

On the Power of Healing

Florence Nightingale began modern nursing during the Crimean War of the mid-nineteenth century. The "Lady with the Lamp" was a tireless worker. But besides being extraordinarily practical, she saw her work in a very spiritual way as well.

"Nursing – healing – is an art," she wrote. "And if it is to be made an art, it requires as exclusive a devotion, as hard a preparation as any painter's or sculptor's work. For what is having to do with dead canvas or cold marble compared with having to do with the living temple of God's spirit. It is one of the Fine Arts. I had almost said the finest of the Fine Arts."

Whatever you do has a religious element because all that is human is tied to the spiritual. Consider the most down to earth matters in your life. Open your eyes and look at them with God's vision. Open your eyes.

Jesus said…'Blessed are the eyes that see what you see!' (Luke 10:23)

Divine Physician, use me as Your instrument to heal the wounds of Your people.

Is Today the Day?

Playwright Moss Hart *(You Can't Take it With You; The Man Who Came to Dinner)* grew up in the Bronx.

He spent his earliest working days in a furrier's vault, yearning for a life in the glow of Broadway.

After nearly three years with the furrier, at the tender age of 16, he decided one morning that he would never return. Mustering all his courage, he stopped by the theatrical office where his neighbor, George Steinberg, held Hart's dream job: errand boy.

A short-tempered secretary told Hart that Steinberg had quit that very day. "In a dazzling moment, I saw the finger of fate beckoning me on," Hart later wrote. He got the job and continued seizing opportunities throughout the rest of his career.

Have a dream? Create the opportunities to make it real.

You need endurance. (Hebrews 10:36)

How are You calling me, today, Lord?

Outspoken Woman, Caring Journalist

Rossana Rosado seems to be making a career out of breaking barriers and making her voice heard. Rosado a former reporter, was at 38 named publisher of *El Diario-La Prensa,* one of the major Spanish-language publications in the United States.

A passionate woman, she admired that quality in her mentor the late Manuel de Dios Unanue, editor-in-chief of *El Diario,* who was murdered in 1992 by a member of a Colombian drug cartel. She says her mentor's journalistic style was "passion on the front page." She adds, "I was very comfortable with that."

Are you comfortable with taking a stand – being passionate – on one or more issues of importance to you? It's the only way your opinion will be heard; problems solved; actions for good taken.

I must cry out. I must shout. (Jeremiah 20:8)

God grant us the courage to do what needs to be done.

An American-Just-Outside-of-Paris

After spending a quarter-century in France, first as a reporter, then as husband, father and citizen of Bourron-Marlotte, Rudolph Chelminski is resigned to the fact that, as Americans, he and his family will never totally meld into the society.

"We have been accepted," he observes. "We're grateful for that and don't ask for anything more."

But he received much more from his neighbors on June 6, 1994. The town's mayor invited Chelminski to be the guest of honor at a ceremony in memory of the Normandy invasion 50 years earlier. "I was only a boy when D-Day happened," he said. But the townspeople honored Chelminski as a surrogate "for all the G.I.'s lying under those symmetrical white crosses in Colleville-sur-Mer."

Large or little, we all have a place in history.

Love your neighbor as yourself. (Leviticus 19:18)

Lord, every aspect of my life has purpose. Help me to always honor all that I am.

Toward a Marriage Made in Heaven

Ask most married people, "How is your relationship going?" and you'll probably hear something like, "It's okay, I guess." Small grievances are often the ones that interfere most with marital happiness. If you let go of the little things, you'll find new ways to nurture one another. Consider these strategies:

Stop adding up all you are doing and your partner is not.

Take charge of your own happiness. You can make yourself happy. That takes the pressure off your partner.

Recognize your quirks and your partner's. Learn to live with them.

Learn to accept apologies and to make them.

Make time with your spouse a priority.

The truth is that any marriage – from troubled to terrific can grow in love with a little extra effort.

**Love one another deeply from the heart.
(1 Peter 1:22)**

Your love for us, Creator, is infinite and unconditional. Help us always to remember this.

Devotion Recalled

She was a sweet, smart, and dedicated woman. Miss Angie Post of Wilton, Connecticut, was the teacher at the Hurlbutt Street School, the last one-room schoolhouse in town. The students she shaped, senior citizens now, remember her fondly.

How is it that people and events from the 1920s can still influence today? Was it the way Miss Post sat with one to review lessons? Was it promoting older students to assistants, reinforcing their own learning as they passed it along to younger students?

Perhaps it is the memory of parents who supported Miss Post's efforts by providing warm loaves of bread and big pots of soup for lunch.

It's not unusual for a fine teacher to be memorable. The fact is, every one of us can affect tomorrow's memories for someone.

In the memory of virtue is immortality.
(Wisdom of Solomon 4:1)

I know Your path holds delights, Spirit of Love; help me find it, so I can share Your joy with others.

Baseball's Lessons

Writer Bernie Sheahan is an avid baseball fan. But more than just hours of enjoyment, the game gives her lessons for life.

One player Sheahan admires is pitcher Orel Hershiser, now retired, because of his athletic skill and because he is never afraid to talk in public about his love for his wife and children and God. Sheahan found his remarks "eloquent and graceful."

Grace-full is what she means. "Baseball is nothing if not a game of grace, a forgiving sport that reminds us...there's always a next pitch, a next inning and a next game."

When you need sustenance during life's trials, remember baseball and the Bible. Sheahan, for instance, recalls the book of Lamentations: "His mercies are new every morning." Or, in the language of baseball, "there's always another season."

This I call to mind, and therefore I have hope: The steadfast love of the Lord never ceases, His mercies...are new every morning. (Lamentations 3:21-22,23)

Give us the strength to go on, God, our refuge, no matter what.

Living for Lava

Haraldur Sigurdsson has hacked through jungles, paddled across boiling lakes, gone to the seafloor in submarines, and camped in the crater of an active volcanic.

Sigurdsson is a volcanologist who has spent his life picking through stones coughed up by volcanoes to discover the earth's workings as well as unearthing clues to human history hidden in ash.

Sigurdsson first came under the spell of volcanoes growing up in Iceland. Now living in Rhode Island, he likens himself to a detective picking through a crime scene, reconstructing the history of eruptions through what they've left behind. The joy in fieldwork remains in "turning over every rock, cracking each open to see what's inside, and just trying to understand the earth."

Increase your knowledge of your – our – home, Earth.

The sea looked and fled; Jordan turned back. The mountains skipped like rams, the hills like lambs. ...at the presence of the God of Jacob. (Psalm 114:3-4,7)

In confusion and fear, I turn to You, Lord, for guidance and for hope.

You've Got to Start Somewhere

Susan Abbott and her children were driving past a rundown church in Henderson, North Carolina, when they saw an elderly man hard at work. Something moved her to stop and ask if he needed help.

The man, Rev. Winston Blackwell, the 74-year-old pastor of the small old Saint Paul AME Zion church, smiled and said: "I need so much help, where do I start?" Rev. Blackwell had been using a handsaw to cut down several 75-foot trees that threatened to fall on the uninsured church and that blocked a donated steeple from being erected.

Susan Abbott and her children left the clergyman and returned with a chainsaw and her husband, Randy. By nightfall, they had sawed five trees into firewood. Rev. Blackwell has since made them honorary members of his church.

An offer of help: when was the last time you made one?

My help comes from the Lord. (Psalm 121.2)

When I call to You for help, Father, hear my voice and answer me.

A Two-Way Street

Communication may be a two-way street filled with roadblocks, but the simple fact is this: the better we listen, the more we hear.

Here are listening styles which impede hearing:

A mind reader wonders, "What is this person *really* thinking or feeling?"

A filterer listens selectively, hearing only what he or she wants to hear.

A dreamer drifts off and must ask the speaker to repeat.

An identifier refers everything to personal experience.

A placater agrees with everything to be nice or to avoid conflict.

Do you change the subject so quickly that it indicates you're not interested in what's being said? Hearing but quickly discounting what's said is also a form of derailing the conversation.

Be an active listener. Roadblocks will disappear.

Listen to advice and accept instruction. (Proverbs 19:20)

Spirit, guide me to close my mouth and open my mind.

What's a Nice Lawyer Like You...

John Rosenberg first went to David, Kentucky, to help families in a tenant-landlord dispute.

More than a quarter of a century later, he is still there. In that time he has helped build playgrounds, a science center, a school. He has also helped people rebuild their lives. His law firm gives priority to cases involving domestic violence.

This is a great accomplishment for Rosenberg who, on his arrival in the area, was labeled a radical. Now he's hailed as someone who has done "wonderful things for eastern Kentucky."

Rosenberg was born in Germany in 1931 just as the Nazis were seizing power. He and his family managed to escape to the U.S. on one of the last ships. For him the reason for his service is simple: to make life better for everyone.

What motivates you to service and good deeds?

You shall love your neighbor as yourself: I am the Lord. (Leviticus 19:18)

Within my soul, Master, I carry the spark of Your love. Help me to use that gift wisely and for the good of others.

Patriotism and the Flag

"It's just a piece of cloth, but it means so much," says Barry Kessler who owns a flag, banner and sign company. He adds, "In this business you get a feel for...what patriotism is all about. The American flag captures the blood and guts of all these people that died for freedom."

You know that the U.S. flag now has 50 stars, one for each state in the Union and 13 stripes, seven red and six white, which represent the 13 original colonies. Did you know that there is an etiquette for displaying flags? Flags at half-staff signify mourning. Flags should be raised and lowered carefully, without touching the ground. There is a precise way to fold them.

Flags should mean something special to us, but no more so than the country we hold dear and its people, our neighbors.

Pay...taxes to whom taxes are due, revenue to whom revenue is due, respect to whom respect is due, honor to whom honor is due.
(Romans 13:7)

God bless the nation we love!

Dads Matter

Today, the number of fathers solely responsible for the care of their children is growing at almost twice that of mothers.

The media often mentions the absentee dad, the deadbeat dad, the career-at-all-costs dad. Yet millions of single fathers are creating a new model of fatherhood.

One retail executive's wife abandoned him and their two children. To have childcare flexibility, the father took a job in a produce market. A contractor drove 12 hours every other weekend to be with his son. After 14 years he won sole custody.

Children need two parents to be there and to care about them. The love of fathers and mothers is irreplaceable. Show your love today and everyday.

Honor your father by word and deed. (Sirach 3:8)

Father of all, surround us with Your love; clothe us with Your peace.

Passing on the Faith

Bringing your children to weekly worship may not be enough if you are serious about passing on your religious tradition to your children. Focus on the Family holds conferences to give parents fun and practical tools.

Spokesman John Trent explains that "We felt there had to be more parents could do beyond taking the kids to church or sending them to Sunday school." The Bible instructs parents to "train up a child in the way he should go," and "we want to empower parents and get them to say, 'I can do this'."

Everyday routines present opportunities to pass on spiritual truths. Steer discussions toward the spiritual whether at dinner or while driving. Consider a weekly family night which can include spiritual elements. Say bedtime prayers together.

Take the time to open your heart to your youngsters and they will be more receptive to what you have to say. The result can be your children's spiritual growth and your own.

Train yourself in godliness. (1 Timothy 4:7)

Help me build spiritual bridges, Creator.

Love Conquers All

Lane Anderson and Brett Taylor were planning to be married at Calvary (Episcopal) Parish, Tarboro, North Carolina. Then the Tar River rose to a 500-year flood stage.

They decided to be married at once, "come hell or high water," before the church was submerged in water. People were told, "come as you are." The bride wore pearls and soggy, cut-off bib overalls; the groom, khaki shorts. Both were barefoot. The priest wore hunting boots with his vestments. The church was lit by candles. Several attendants as well as the bride's parents couldn't reach the church.

Still, the Rev. Bill Smyth called the wedding "happy and fun, with a certain style and grace and dignity; a marvelous service of worship."

Especially in matters of the heart, where there's a will there's a way. Determination and perseverance are vital.

Love is strong as death, passion fierce as the grave. ...Many waters cannot quench love, neither can floods drown it.
(Song of Solomon 8:6,7)

With You, nothing will deter me, Loving Lord.

One Woman's Crusade

Alsen, Louisiana, is at the end of the industrial corridor known as "Cancer Alley." Home to several chemical industries and a hazardous waste incinerator, the town's mostly black citizens are at risk from the pollution.

Florence Robinson, a local biology professor, awoke one day in 1988 with a crippling headache. After a winter of illnesses that led to hospitalization, she started looking for the possible causes. She "realized that people around me were sick or dying." and that Alsen residents suffered more than their share of illnesses.

Knowing "that something had to change," Robinson founded the Communities at Risk Coalition Network to help citizens who live near hazardous waste sites.

Florence Robinson wants to keep industries "honest." Her motto teaches a valuable lesson. "People don't understand that not only can they make a difference, it's their responsibility to do so."

Be rich in good works. (1 Timothy 6:18)

May I make a difference for right, just and merciful God.

The Coach

"Reputation is what you are perceived to be. Character is what you really are," said basketball coach John Wooden. During his UCLA tenure, his teams won 10 NCAA championships. Between January of 1971 and January of 1974, they won 88 straight games.

Of his 180 players, Wooden knows the whereabouts of 172. Most of them still telephone him. He would tell them, "Discipline yourself, and other won't need to. Never lie, never cheat, never steal. Earn the right to be proud and confidant."

They all knew that when they played for him they played by his rules: acknowledge your teammates, use no profanity, and treat your opponent with respect.

As one writer put it, John Wooden was a man from whom anyone could learn about life and love.

I turn my feet to Your decrees; I hurry and do not delay to keep Your commandments. (Psalm 119:59-60)

Guide me to always choose the right and moral path, Jesus.

Eating and Sharing

The modern family tends to view food as gasoline for the body. The frantic pace of life makes dinnertime a kind of refueling. We forget that it can be a restorative ritual for both body and spirit.

Do you miss a traditional family meal? With a little effort and a few pointers, you don't have to any more.

"Dinner was a...togetherness, for better or worse," writes Greg Erlandson, a father of three children, of the family meals of his youth. He and his wife have restored dinner time for their family.

Erlandson advises banning the television and ignoring the phone during mealtime. Also, a schedule helps. If not dinner together every night, then at least once a week. Accept dinner as a family priority. And let the stories, laughter, discussions and eating begin!

When He was at the table with them, He took bread, blessed and broke it, and gave it to them. ...and they recognized Him. (Luke 24:30,31)

Help us share ourselves with family and friends as You did at the supper at Emmaus, Risen Jesus.

Not Just Women

The assumption is that anorexia is a women's eating disorder. Yet one of six anorexics are men.

Dr. Thomas Holbrook, a recovering anorexic, traces his struggle with food to lifelong insecurities and feelings of inadequacy. He exercised obsessively and limited himself to a single daily salad for 12 years. "I was terrified of being fat."

Since diagnosing his disorder in 1998, Dr. Holbrook has achieved a healthy weight, co-authored, *Making Weight: Men's Conflicts with Food, Weight, Shape & Appearance,* and become director of a Wisconsin hospital's eating disorder center.

Dr. Holbrook says it's very hard for men "to accept that they care so much about how their bodies look." He helps them by telling men that he understands what they're going through.

Empathy is key to helping others. What can you share?

We...have a high priest who...in every respect has been tested as we are, yet without sin. (Hebrews 4:15)

Holy Spirit, may I treat my body as Your own dwelling.

The Sounds of Louis Armstrong

Does Louis Armstrong get his due as a jazz great, or is he given short shrift by those who rightly praise the genius of Duke Ellington or the innovations of Charlie Parker and Dizzy Gillespie?

Writing in *Civilization* magazine, David Samuels argues that Armstrong's wild, inventive jazz in the 1920's ignited an ongoing musical revolution. Armstrong's jazz was "formed by the collisions between folk tradition and classical form, the sound of symphony orchestras and the songs of Southern Blacks, old vocal traditions and the new technology of movies, radio and records."

The music wasn't black or white, "if music can have a color," writes Samuels. It was truly multicultural, "crossing settled boundaries of race and region, of high and low culture."

There can be no question that this giant of jazz brought pleasure to his audiences and still does. Whatever you do, do it with all your heart.

Wine and music gladden the heart. (Sirach 40:20)

Thank you, Creator, for the music in our lives.

Driving for Independence

In many United States communities, not having a car is akin to not being independent.

"I may be 81, but I like my independence. I just couldn't sit at home," said one retired English teacher. "Since a friend told me about the Independent Transportation Network (ITN), I have been able to come and go when I want...to keep a full life."

Katherine Freund, founded ITN in Maine in 1995 because without alternatives "vital people end up isolated and depressed – or still driving when they shouldn't be."

ITN is a door-to-door car service for seniors and visually impaired people who can't afford taxis, who need more flexible service than that provided by buses or who can't always rely on relatives or friends. ITN uses volunteer drivers to keep rides affordable and offers "gift of mobility" gift certificates. Drivers and passengers provide one another companionship

What local problem can you address?

Bear one another's burdens. (Galatians 6:2)

Inspire urban planners and architects to design more human-scale cities and towns, God.

A Child's View of the World

"The things I believe most now are the things called fairy tales. ...They are not fantasies: compared with them other things are fantastic." So writes G. K. Chesterton, the early twentieth century British author, about the lost connection between childhood and adulthood.

What has been lost? For Chesterton it is the joy of discovering infinite possibilities in the ordinary. He chides the adult for getting bored with monotony, urging each of us to see its fairytale potential. The adult is unimpressed by the leaf being green, for example, "because it could never have been anything else." Why couldn't it have been any color, Chesterton demands.

Children, he observes, love to repeat simple things. They love to be thrown into the air a hundred times. The adult gets tired. The child does not, and that vitality is something every adult should try to rekindle.

Unless you change and become like children, you will never enter the kingdom of heaven. (Matthew 18:3)

Jesus of Nazareth, help me find my child-like-ness, not my child-ish-ness.

Does Your Kitchen Talk Yet?

The Massachusetts Institute of Technology (MIT) is known for its expertise in, well, technology. Achievements start with ideas, lots of ideas. In early stages of research, all are entertained.

Some of MIT's creative minds are working on a so-called "Counter Intelligence" project to develop and test products for the kitchen-of-the-future. There's a Talking Oven Mitt, with its computer circuits, which lets you know when you reach into the oven that your roast is "ready to eat!"

The oven mitt's inventor, Ted Selker, has other items up his sleeve. He has an idea for a salt detector that might be put into a spatula, for instance, to alert those on low-sodium diets.

The lab also created a microwave oven that reads the bar code on a package. It weighs the food item and "nukes" it perfectly.

Creativity is a wonderful gift from God. Use it well.

I called on God, and the spirit of wisdom came to me. (Wisdom of Solomon 7:7)

Holy Spirit, guide us to use technology wisely.

What Your Dog Can Teach You

It is well known that most people only absorb a portion of what they hear. The same is true for seeing.

In his book *Man Meets Dog,* Konrad Lorenz, the Nobel Prize winning behaviorist, shows how much one can learn from careful observation.

Lorenz describes a host of dog cues that he was able to understand through patience and empathy. The ruffled mane and flat ears of his dog Stasi tell Lorenz, returning from a long absence, that his companion is unwelcoming. But after a cathartic wolf-like howl, Stasi greets him with wild exuberance and is back to her normal self.

Lorenz could have jumped the gun and misinterpreted Stasi's initial unfriendliness as a permanent change, but instead he correctly understood it as a response to imagined abandonment.

Thoughtful observation can often save us from making the wrong conclusions about our animal – and human – friends.

Observe carefully what is before you. (Proverbs 23:1)

Sharpen my senses, Lord, that I may be more fully present to others, to You, and to Your world.

Mission of Mercy

American psychiatrist Jim Gordon, director of the Center for Mind-Body Medicine in Washington, D.C., traveled to war-ravaged Kosovo nine times. Using a variety of holistic healing methods, Dr. Gordon tries to help many of the estimated 500,000 people suffering from post-traumatic stress disorder.

His credentials are decidedly mainstream, yet he believes that the physiological effects of exercise, dietary changes, herbal supplements and psychotherapy can transform even chronically depressed patients. "We have a great and largely untapped capacity to improve on our own health," says the Harvard-educated doctor.

Dr. Gordon's methods may seem simplistic. But in a country with almost no health system, all help is welcomed. His is a hands-on, gentle, approach to healing. As one woman said after speaking to him, "I'm feeling better. It felt good to talk."

We participate in God's healing when we care for others

Recovery lies in the hands of physicians. (Sirach 38:13)

Redeemer, help me be a whole-souled listener.

Surviving Evil

During World War II, Pepi Deutsch couldn't have known she'd live for 101 years. But she knew she was a survivor.

Mrs. Deutsch got herself and her teenage daughter, Clara, through brutalities suffered at Nazi hands in various concentration camps. She protected her daughter as best she could. For Clara's 17th birthday, she'd hoarded three slices of bread, spread them with marmalade and created a cake.

Her own mother, husband, son and more than 30 other relatives weren't so fortunate. They perished in the Holocaust.

Still she never lost faith despite the horrors. Pepi Deutsch said the slaughter of six million Jews "was not God's fault. (It) was done by monsters."

Sadly, not monsters, but people. People who misused their God-given gift of free will to choose hatred instead of love.

**Love does no wrong to a neighbor.
(Romans 13:10)**

Jesus, forgive us for forgetting that You lived and died a faithful Son of the Torah.

A Tennis Ace Serves Kids

Andre Agassi has never strayed from his Las Vegas roots. Since 1994, the tennis ace has helped disadvantaged kids in Las Vegas find ways to grow in sports, the arts and education through his Andre Agassi Charitable Foundation.

Even as a very young man, Agassi wanted to put his wealth and celebrity to good use. He wanted to give kids an opportunity "to make better decisions for themselves."

Agassi's charity funds such projects as eight fine arts scholarships at the University of Nevada at Las Vegas, and a special-needs medical cottage at the Child Haven protective custody center. Seeing the youngsters he helps, "you get to really reap the benefits of the difference you're making," says Agassi.

There are an infinite number of ways in which you can help, improve, repair. Put your talents and resources to work for others.

Give thanks to God. (Romans 14:6)

Who, Lord God, needs my assistance?

Our Nation's Living Symbol

After a three-decade effort, the American bald eagle, our country's living symbol, is no longer on the endangered species list.

When the Continental Congress put the bald eagle at the center of the Great Seal of the United States, there were as many as 500,000 eagles in the skies over North America. After hunting, loss of prey and habitat, and pesticide use, only 417 breeding pairs remained by 1963.

The pesticide D.D.T. was banned in 1972. The Endangered Species Act was passed a year later. And the bald eagle began its recovery. Now 5,800 breeding pairs are legally protected.

We are God's stewards. It is up to us to protect His creation with wisdom and determination.

It is required of stewards that they be found trustworthy. (1 Corinthians 4:2)

Father, bless our efforts to undo past damage to Your creation and to make the future brighter.

Harry Coleburn Buys a Bear

When veterinarian Harry Coleburn left Winnipeg to enlist in the Canadian Army at the beginning of World War I, he couldn't resist purchasing a bear cub from a hunter who was selling him at a train station. His regiment soon adopted the little cub and named him Winnie, in honor of Coleburn's hometown.

Coleburn left the animal at the London Zoo for safekeeping when he was called to duty in France. Four years later, the playful bear had become such an attraction that Coleburn decided to leave him at the zoo. There he entertained visitors for years.

Among those visitors was the Milne family. Young Christopher Robin was so taken with Winnie, he renamed his beloved stuffed bear Edward for him (Pooh came from another animal he admired, a swan). The rest, as they say, is history: A.A. Milne soon started writing Winnie the Pooh stories inspired by his son's little companion.

Not every seemingly insignificant decision will bring happiness to people around the world, but then again, you never know.

The discerning person looks to wisdom. (Proverbs 17:24)

Deepen my trust, God, that You are present in each moment.

I Do...Forgive

People hurt each other. Married people are no different.

Two programs of the Catholic Church, Marriage Encounter and Retrouvaille, emphasize reconciliation in the husband-wife relationship.

At a Marriage Encounter weekend, there is an intense "course in communication." It often has an amazing impact on the couples, in many cases bringing healing and reconciliation to lives filled with pain and remorse.

While Marriage Encounter helps make good marriages better, a Retrouvaille (meaning "rediscovery") weekend – with a three-month follow up program – helps troubled couples make their way back together. At least one of the presenting couples at such a weekend had experienced separation before deciding to start again.

Reconciliation and forgiveness call for honest communication. Strive to be open and caring in your relationships.

Let marriage be held in honor. (Hebrews 13:4)

Show us Your mercy and Your kindness, Master. Forgive us when we turn from You and one another.

Making Noise

Catherine Phiri can't keep silent. In fact, this nurse from Malawi won't stop talking until everyone in her African homeland has a fighting chance against HIV-AIDS.

Phiri contracted the AIDS virus from her husband. He died from it. At the time, Malawi's government refused to allow any public discussion of HIV or AIDS. By the time a democratically elected government came into power in 1994, Phiri, like many others, was already a victim of the silence.

These days, Phiri uses her slim earnings as a consultant on HIV-AIDS for testing, counseling and moral support for those with the virus. She is also raising six children, four of them AIDS orphans she has adopted.

No one can afford to keep silent about this life and death issue. When lives are at stake, speak up. It's your responsibility.

A Samaritan...came near him; and when he saw him, he was moved with pity. (Luke 10:33)

Divine Physician, inspire HIV-AIDS researchers and all who support their efforts.

Star Spangled Survivor

Did you know that the flag Francis Scott Key wrote about in "The Star Spangled Banner" still exists today?

The giant flag, one of the Smithsonian Institution's proudest treasures, measures 42 by 30 feet, with 15 stars and 15 stripes (the number of stripes didn't revert to 13 – for the original 13 colonies – until 1818).

Currently, a team of conservators is working to restore the fragile fabric, inching carefully around it, examining every flaw and thread. Complete restoration of this precious national treasure is expected to be finished in 2002.

In its way, the fragility of that flag that flew over Fort McHenry during the War of 1812 symbolizes democracy. If we don't tend to it, care for it and work to preserve it, we could lose it.

You were called to freedom. (Galatians 5:13)

I pray, dear Lord, for those who live in oppression. I am grateful for the freedom I hope I shall never take for granted.

Giving Away, Giving Back

Whether they like it or not, professional athletes are role models for young people. So when they make an extra effort to reach out, it means so much.

Tampa Buccaneer linebacker Derrick Brooks started his Brooks Bunch program through local Boys and Girls Clubs and gave out tickets to football games.

But he wanted to do more. To motivate youngsters to focus on achieving a goal, he has offered trips to Atlanta and Washington, D.C. Then Brooks decided that he wanted to visit Africa and bring along twenty teens. Those who hoped to go had to keep up their regular school work and attendance. They also had to attend special classes on the history and culture of Africa, keep a journal on what they were learning and finally submit an essay on why they should be chosen. Derrick Brooks led the memorable trip and plans to do it again.

Think about how you can exert a positive influence.

Be rich in good works. (1 Timothy 6:18)

Someone is counting on me. Savior of all, don't let me fail.

To the Moon, Dolores...

The next time you see the moon, think of Dolores Black.

She was chosen to sew the American flag that Neil Armstrong put on the moon during the Apollo 11 lunar landing on July 20, 1969.

Black sewed the three-foot-long double-faced nylon flag with embroidered stars when she was an employee at Eder Flag Corporation in Milwaukee, Wisconsin. The whole project took a month because, says Black, she wanted every stitch to be perfect.

Only years later did Black start talking about her part in history. She wrote down the story for her grandchildren. "I had never talked about it because…it was simply part of my job," Black says. "What a great honor it was for me."

Sewn into one of the seams of that flag is her signature. Where have you left your mark?

The memory of the righteous is a blessing. (Proverbs 10:7)

Father, You have written Your law in our hearts; give us the grace and strength to do Your will in all we do.

Creating a More Interesting YOU

If your life feels boring, don't blame life. Only YOU can make your life interesting. Consider these four suggestions.

Cultivate a diverse group of friends. Surround yourself with people different from you. Their energy may rub off.

Find your life's work. God calls your best self to your best work and your best work makes you interesting. What do you want to do more than anything else: parenting or gardening or building or teaching or writing? Over a lifetime, it could be many things. Follow your interest wherever it leads.

Educate yourself. Keeping yourself interesting depends in many ways on what you know. Read. Volunteer. Go to museums and plays. Take classes. Travel.

Take sides. But pick your battles wisely and take sides only on issues that touch your strongest beliefs. Others have a right to their own opinions.

God has given us so much. Enjoy and appreciate it!

Decide with equity. (Isaiah 11:4)

Guide me, Master, along the path to You.

Time for Togetherness

The family reunion: Hugs and laughter, grilled food and softball games if you're lucky enough to have someone to orchestrate what can be a major endeavor.

Publisher Edith Wagner of *Reunions Magazine* estimates that the over 200,000 annual family reunions in the U.S. have become a $1 billion industry.

Some reunions are so large they're more like conventions with genealogy workshops, performances and lectures. Others gather at resorts for several days of togetherness. But no matter how or where it happens, the important thing is that it happens.

According to Wagner, the fact that people want to stay in touch and "give the kids a sense of where they come from and how they fit in" accounts for the growing popularity of reunions.

Adds Donna Beasley, author of *The Family Reunion Planner*, "All you really need is a family and folks ready to get together."

Make the time for celebration in your life.

I will be the God of all the families...and they shall be My people. (Jeremiah 31:1)

Let us celebrate all You have called us to be, Father.

Charting Your Course

Errol Richardson has his dream job. Working for the Hagstrom Map Company, he specializes in New York City.

The native of Trinidad knows every nook and cranny of the city that never sleeps.

How does he do it? Richardson listens to the news. He reads the newspaper. He responds to those who point out discrepancies. He has also become familiar with the history of the city and has been known to wander around checking out his maps first hand. He claims he cannot get lost.

"There is a major road running through every neighborhood," he told the *New York Times*. "Once you know where that major road is, you can find your way."

Is it time to update your life's map? Consider your history, factor in current circumstances, listen to others and seek the Spirit of God.

If I...settle at the farthest limits of the sea, even there Your hand shall lead me, and Your right hand shall hold me fast. (Psalm 139:9-10)

Help me to enjoy life's journey, Lord. Don't let me wander from Your road.

Sister, Administrator, War Hero

It takes courage to serve God's people.

Jane Keating arrived in New York from Ireland in July of 1852. Within a few years she became a Sister of St. Joseph, taking the name Sister Mary de Chantal.

The Civil War brought great change to her life. She was sent to Wheeling, West Virginia to run a hospital. She made up for her lack of training with her courage.

West Virginia had declared itself a Union state, and while Mother Mary took the Oath of Allegiance required by the government, she was unwilling to turn away anyone in need of hospitalization. She even hid Confederate soldiers in the basement of both the hospital and convent in order to treat them.

According to letters received by family members, Mother Mary even chose to bury one of the nuns who had died of smallpox in the middle of the night rather than report her death and risk a search of the hospital.

Courage defined this woman's life. Does it define yours?

Take courage; I have conquered. (John 16:33)

Spirit of Fortitude, give us the courage to do what we know is right.

Stripes or Spots?

Are you a cuttlefish?

They are masters of both communication and disguise. Like chameleons they can change the color of their skin to match their surroundings, but they can also modify its texture. And their repertoire is far more vast: they can shift from speckled to whorled to black, to white, to brown to gray, to pink, to red, and iridescent. Each mutation takes less than a second.

But for all of their adaptability, cuttlefish are invertebrates, that is spineless.

Many of us adapt our positions to fit those with whom we are conversing. We may find ourselves speaking unkindly of others when they are not present. We may secure our position with friends by seeming to espouse ideas we know to be false.

Are you true to yourself, your standards? Or are you a cuttlefish?

Be courageous and valiant. (2 Samuel 13:28)

Dear God, help me know myself and to be true to myself.

What Will You Choose to See Today?

Nell Musolf called impatiently to her 6-year-old son Hank, frustrated that he was lagging behind her at the mall. "I can't hurry, Mom," he told her. "I'm being aware of this place."

The woman looked around the tired old building, the worn floor and the boarded up shops. Hank was touching the cream-colored walls, running his fingers along an old wooden banister, enjoying the warmth of the sun on his face near a ficus tree. "I'm in the jungle!" he announced.

Realizing her son's wisdom, Nell Musolf asked him what else he was aware of. "Everything!" he replied. And she suddenly realized how long it had been since she had noticed much of anything at all.

Tuning into her son's conversation more carefully, she became aware of exactly where she was in the universe. "And," she said, "I liked it."

How aware are you as you go about your daily activities? Make an effort and you just might surprise yourself.

Give thanks to the Lord. (1 Chronicles 16:8)

Thank You, Lord, for where I am today.

Not So Cut and Dry

In David Hurst Thomas' book, *Skull Wars,* the history of American anthropology is shown in a new light.

Scientists' efforts over the years sometimes included harsh, even inhumane, treatment of Native Americans. Yet, the book is much more than a litany of scientific injustices. Thomas also tells how anthropologists led the way in debunking racist theories that "ranked" human beings. He mentions an anthropologist who fought passionately for the rights of some Native Americans to retain sovereignty of their own land and water.

He suggests that scientists "draw some lessons from the past. Perhaps we can rediscover a more human side to our science and come to value once again the importance of face-to-face relationships with those whose ancestors we wish to study."

History is as complex as the human beings who weave it. There's always more than one side to every story.

I desired to know the truth. (Daniel 7:19)

Help me dig deeply for the truth, Blessed Trinity.

Giving Kids a Place to Call Home

Debrah Constance dropped out of high school, was an alcoholic and survived abuse and three divorces.

She says, "With these sterling qualifications, how could I change my own life, let alone the lives of thousands of children?" Yet years of employment, a wonderful son and good friends helped. And she says, "no matter what happened...it couldn't be much worse than what I'd already been through – or the risks those children faced."

After three years' sobriety and using her experience with AA, she paired students with volunteers from her real estate company. The effort grew into "A Place Called Home," a student service/recreation/education center that provides a haven from the streets. Volunteers tutor in sports, arts and crafts, and other activities.

"Can one person make a difference?" Asks Debrah Constance "In spite of obstacles, shortcomings and impossible odds...absolutely!"

Your individual impact is unique, individual and limitless.

Give relief to the afflicted. (2 Thessalonians 1:7)

God, give me the courage to make a difference in the world.

A Mission as His Mission

When Gerald Miller agreed to become administrator of California's Mission San Juan Capistrano, he expected to remain in the position for less than a year. The former investment banker's task was to help "the mission figure out how to repay a $3 million loan used for seismic retrofitting and to repair the chapel."

Built in 1806, the mission's Great Stone Church stood for only six years before most of it was destroyed in an earthquake. Today, 500,000 visitors a year still visit the crumbling link to California's past. Miller has now spent more than six years working to secure the mission's future, overseeing a conservation plan that will preserve it for generations to come.

Miller says: "We hope that the missions, which are unique to this part of the world, can be our most articulate means of describing our multiethnic heritage."

Do you believe in the importance of what you do?

I delight to do Your will. (Psalm 40:8)

Holy Spirit, may I pursue Your will with passion and vigor.

Miracle in a Jelly Jar

Eight-year-old Tess listened to her mother and father talk about her very sick brother Andrew. With no money for expensive surgery, Tess heard her father say, "Only a miracle can save him."

Tess immediately took her glass jelly jar of money, all $1.11, and went to a nearby drug store. Tess told the pharmacist all about Andrew. And she asked if he sold miracles.

"We don't sell miracles," said the pharmacist, dismissing the child. But his brother who was visiting interrupted and asked how much Tess had in the jar. When she told him, he said, "Well that's the exact price of a miracle for little brothers." The pharmacist's brother was neurosurgeon Dr. Carlton Armstrong—just the help little Andrew needed. Dr. Armstrong performed the much-needed operation without charge.

A miracle is priceless. So is offering a helping hand.

Do not neglect to do good. (Hebrews 13:16)

Father, show me the way to help my brothers and sisters.

It All Begins With One Person

When Elisabeth Bing was herself of child-bearing age, natural childbirth was not an accepted practice. Yet she spearheaded the crusade that made natural childbirth an option for women everywhere.

"We're not lying flat on our backs," says Mrs. Bing. "The father, or anybody else, can be there. We fought for years on end for that. And now its commonplace."

Bing, who fled Nazi Germany in 1933, taught the natural childbirth classes that were considered "revolutionary" in her younger days well into her 80s. She helped found Lamaze International which is named for a doctor who studied breathing exercises for women in labor.

Every individual has the opportunity to influence and benefit the lives of many others. Take advantage of the chances to do good that come your way every day.

The midwives feared God; they did not do as the king of Egypt commanded them, but they let the boys live. (Exodus 1:17)

Give me the strength to serve others, Lord of life.

Your Wish Is Their Command

Never mind convenience. The world wide web has taken commerce a step further. You can buy just about anything customized to your fancy with the touch of a button (and a credit card number).

If you're a college teacher, one publisher will print a customized textbook containing excerpts and articles of your choosing. The print run is determined by the number of your students.

An eyeglass manufacturer will make customized rimless eyeglasses contoured to the shape of your face.

One-on-one marketing, giving you just what you want, seems to be one of the hottest marketing spins today.

In life, attention to detail and flexibility are just as vital. Stay open to new ideas – and old values.

Pay attention! (Job 20:2)

Lord, let me be flexible in business and personal life, so that I may respond positively to the day's challenges.

Bringing the Law to Death Row

Elisabeth Semel, a court-appointed attorney for death row inmates, describes her work as "in crisis mode all the time."

With dozens of death row inmates across the country who lack representation, Semel is continually looking for volunteer attorneys. And, as deadlines for filing appeals near, the need for representation virtually becomes a life-or-death situation.

How does Semel respond when people say she's defending convicted felons, even murderers? "A human being is always more than the worst thing he's ever done," she believes.

Forgiveness is never easy. When it is especially difficult, try to see the good in the other person – look beyond his or her transgression.

Forgive us our debts as we also have forgiven our debtors. (Matthew 6:12)

Jesus, help me when the task of forgiving others becomes too heavy for me. And help me in asking forgiveness, as well.

United They Stand

The Anacostia is one of America's most threatened rivers, yet many people may not even know where it is.

Sometimes called Washington D.C.'s "forgotten" river, the Anacostia actually became a dumping ground for garbage some years back.

But activists Robert Boone and Herb Harris believed it could be otherwise. Interestingly, these men mirror the paradox of the river itself: Boone who is white and Harris who is black united to effect change for the river and their community. The Anacostia River is now undergoing a cleanup, and is again showing signs of life.

Together, we can accomplish anything. Consider the ways in which you can override racial and ethnic barriers in your life.

You make springs gush forth...giving drink to every wild animal...By the streams the birds of the air have their habitation.
(Psalm 104:10,11,12)

We need to work to end racial prejudice so that our nation may be united in peace and justice, Spirit of Courage. Aid us.

Remembering to Forget

Some people have a wonderful knack for forgetting old wounds. They refuse to dwell on hurts and instead practice intentional forgetfulness.

One of them was Clara Barton, founder of the American Red Cross. She was renowned for her inability to hold a grudge. A friend once reminded her of an incident years before when someone had been particularly cruel, asking "Don't you remember the wrong that was done to you?"

Clara Barton replied, "No. I distinctly remember forgetting that."

Maybe there is some hurt, some incident that you would be better off putting behind you – for your sake and that of others, as well. If so, make a decision to forget.

As far as the east is from the west, so far He removes our transgressions from us. ...For He knows how we were made. (Psalm 103:12,14)

Holy God, it is painful to live in the past. Push me forward.

Don't Just Stand There...

Gigi Kelly, a nurse at the University of Pittsburgh Medical Center, was understandably upset at the news of yet another abandoned infant. Her heart ached not only for the child, but also for the desperate situation the mother must have faced.

She decided to place a basket and several blankets on the porch of her home in South Park Township. Sharing the idea with a few friends, she discovered they were willing to offer the same alternative. Within three months, nearly five hundred families had followed her example.

Baskets for Babies now publishes a pamphlet that is distributed to churches, pharmacies, crisis centers, and doctors' offices. Women are encouraged to leave an unwanted child at a volunteer's house, ensuring that someone answers the door before they depart, no questions asked.

What small step might you take to assuage pain with love?

Rescue the oppressed, defend the orphan, plead for the widow. (Isaiah 1:17)

Help me, Infant Lord Jesus, to take action to aid women and children in need.

A Town Called Clyde

The upstate New York town of Clyde is trying to transform itself into Clyde-on-the-Erie, tourist magnet. Right now life in Clyde is "boring," says a resident. The Chamber of Commerce and other civic organizations have dwindled. There's no more annual Christmas decoration competition.

Railroad tracks run between the Erie Canal and three-block-long downtown Clyde. And the only dock on the Erie Canal can not accommodate anything much bigger than a rowboat.

Nevertheless, Clyde, halfway between Rochester and Syracuse, continues to pin its hopes for the future on the canal that first gave it life in the 1820s. It was the first stop for westbound barges.

Since 1996 the federal government has backed a "canal corridor initiative." Clyde is one of many small towns trying to renew itself in the face of economic problems.

If it is to succeed it will take planning and hard work. But it must start with hope. Good things always do.

Abound in hope. (Romans 15:13)

Only in You, Creator, can we find the meaning and purpose of our lives.

Family Values, Living Values

The five Pharis sisters were "raised to defend and depend on each other," explains Linda. They bickered, but nobody held a grudge. And "to criticize family to outsiders was unconscionable. Complaints stopped at our front door," says Aularia.

The women credit their Southern-born parents for instilling such strong family values. Manners and perseverance were priorities. "We were told we could do whatever we put our minds to," says Tangra. "Being female or black was no reason to be held back!" Adds Claudia, "I know there's nothing I could do that would make my sisters not love me."

The Pharis sisters are now in their 50s. Aularia is a Los Angeles trial attorney; Linda director of public affairs for a Philadelphia TV station; Claudia is now chief of staff for a congressman; Tangra is a community activist and painter; and Karen is an account executive.

What values, rooted in your childhood, define your life?

Unless the Lord builds the house, those who build it labor in vain. (Psalm 127:1)

Heavenly Father, may I hold fast to the values that bring me closer to You.

In Charge of an Emerald Field

Maria Hernandez is the keeper of the grass, the Great Lawn of New York City's Central Park.

By late 1995, the 55-acre lawn at the center of the Park had become a rutted dust bowl. So the city and the Central Park Conservancy closed it for two years to restore it. They put Hernandez in charge.

She and her crew work hard to keep the lawn clean and pleasant for all. No one who violates that space is exempt – Hernandez once told two mounted police officers to get off her lawn.

For Maria Hernandez, that lawn is part of her own history. She was three when her family moved from Cuba to New York and lived across from the park. "It was my backyard, my playground, my hiding place," she says.

Now she makes sure the emerald field remains that for many others for a long time to come.

Preserve what is beautiful in your community.

Be found trustworthy. (1 Corinthians 4:2)

We are stewards of Your creation, Master. Help us respect and preserve its beauty.

Healing Bodies, Soothing Souls

The Philadelphia Doctors' Chamber Orchestra is the dream come true of a surgeon who wields both baton and scalpel.

Dr. Fawzi Habboushe, who studied medicine at the University of Pennsylvania and conducting at Temple University, formed his first orchestra in about 1978. But he had to put it aside because of family responsibilities.

In 1993, Dr. Habboushe revived his 45-member orchestra. While most of the musicians are health-care professionals, others are teachers, students and retirees. They play at local churches and institutions.

Dr. Habboushe can't say whether music or medicine is more important to him. "I'm immersed more frequently into surgery, and in it I am sure I frequently touch shoulders with God without knowing it." But, adds Dr. Habboushe, "Music is the best medium to God. I see God in Bach. ...Handel is very celestial."

Find time for the joy that comes from caring for body and soul.

Wine and music gladden the heart, but the love of friends is better than either. (Sirach 40:20)

Thank You, Creator, for the gifts we've been blessed with.

"All the Difference"

Feel like you should be in control of your life, but you're not?

Look to the great American poet, Robert Frost for inspiration. His famous poem *The Road Not Taken* is often misunderstood as a kind of praise of the far-seeing individual. The poet recounts coming to a place where a grassy trail divides in two. Imagining a successful life because of choosing one road over another, Frost seems to proudly declare, "I took the one less traveled by, and that has made all the difference."

But he is ironic, since "the passing there had worn (the paths) really about the same." In other words, with no visible difference in the roads, the choice was random.

Big choices in our lives can often seem indistinguishable, but it is how we tread the path once chosen and the actions that we take along the way that really make the difference.

Decide with equity. (Isaiah 11:4)

Guide and inspire our decision making, Holy Spirit.

Can't Stop the Music

Viola Smith would hurl her drumstick onto her drum, then jump up in the air and catch it as it bounced. Roz Cron was well-known for the beautiful, clear tone and distinct phrasing of her alto sax and clarinet.

The two women were among the stars of the all-girl bands that thrived during World War II. After the fighting stopped and the men returned home, many women married and left the bands. Others found their jobs now in the hands of men. But a number kept on making music.

Take Clora Bryant, a gifted trumpeter. "My dad taught me to be aggressive and assertive," she says. "I worked all the time," she noted, including with jazz greats like Johnny Otis and Dizzy Gillespie. Today, in her 70s and recovering from heart surgery, Clora Bryant is still touring, "It's in my blood."

Be assertive in choosing to live the life God wants for you.

A woman who fears the Lord is to be praised. (Proverbs 31:30)

Give me strength, Lord. Help me to realize that You are never far from me.

Heart of Nature's Mystery

Everyday, we learn more about how wondrously complex and elegant the human body is, and how much it shares with God's other creations.

The heart has served as the subject of many a poem. It is a powerful image because it brings life to all the body's cells.

Science has shown that more primitive creatures have cells that are independent of such a central life-giving mechanism. The sponge, for example, has cells that extract oxygen and particles of food from surrounding water.

But more complex animals require a circulatory system that carries nutrients and oxygen throughout the body. Recent discoveries suggest that the heart of creatures as diverse as the fruit fly and the Blue Whale may have gotten its start in the throat of a worm.

Nature's mysteries remind us of our need for humility and our fascinating connection to other creatures and our Creator.

God saw everything He had made, and indeed, it was very good. (Genesis 1:31)

May a tender loving kindness toward all creation be the expression of our gratitude for our lives, Father Creator.

The Old Neighborhood

Al Rapone grew up playing some serious stickball in Astoria, Queens, a section of New York City famous for being a mosaic of immigrant cultures.

Not long ago, at the age of 65, he longed for the simpler days of his youth when "stickball was a way of life." With his brother Peter, then 72, the Rapone brothers decided to stop day-dreaming and do something. They organized a reunion and planned a game with their friends from "the old neighborhood." Many traveled from all over just to make the game.

Sam Cicerale, 71, Rudy Carolla, 64 and Steve Savino, 80, were some of those who took their turn at bat. But their return was not about a childhood game. Says Mr. Carolla, "It's the neighborhood. You get to a certain point in life, roots are comfortable."

Take the initiative in developing your community ties and you'll always have someplace to call home.

Better is a neighbor who is nearby than kindred who are far away. (Proverbs 27:10)

My community and my place in it are gifts from You, O Lord. Thank You.

Persistence Pays Off

A persistent research veterinarian at the Bronx Zoo is credited with helping identify a mysterious ailment that began sickening and in some cases killing New Yorkers in 1999.

The deadly culprit was the West Nile virus. Dr. Tracey S. McNamara had been studying the deaths of large numbers of birds in the Bronx. These were occurring at about the same time humans were being stricken.

The coincidence was "too striking to ignore," said Dr. McNamara. She saw in her research something about the virus which was killing the birds. And, "I knew we had something new."

Dr. McNamara contacted the Center for Disease Control and Prevention in Atlanta with her evidence and suspicions. West Nile virus had been discovered.

Curiosity and persistence pay off and not just in scientific endeavors but in life.

Be persistent whether the time is favorable or unfavorable. (2 Timothy 4:2)

Help me, Jesus, to keep going even when it's hard.

Making a Difference in Mexico

Dr. Kevin Glynn and his wife, a nurse, took a "vacation" in Mexico. But instead of relaxing on the beach they, along with 14 physicians, 16 nurses and 18 support personnel, went to Uruapan, 200 miles west of Mexico City as part of the Mercy Outreach Surgical Team.

There this team of medical professionals completed 217 procedures, ranging from simple cleft-lip repairs to complex reconstruction for burn scars in four days. That's a month's work for an average U.S. hospital.

The Glynns learned many things during their time in Mexico: the value of teamwork; the amazing endurance and trust of their young patients. One particular girl touched them. Before her operation she would hide in her house because of disfiguring facial scars from a burn. Now she enjoys traveling because "I am beautiful."

Reveal the beauty in another's soul through your love.

Do not withhold good...when it is in your power to do it. (Proverbs 3:27)

You created me, Master, to bring Your light and love to those who live in darkness and pain. Thank You.

Fast Forgiveness

If you have ever asked forgiveness and been denied it, you will appreciate the following true story. If you have been the one to withhold forgiveness, you might value it even more.

A mother had a young son who had a knack for getting into trouble for little mishaps. After he was scolded, he would say he was sorry and reach for a hug. His mother started to worry that he thought he was "getting away with it."

Then he did something a bit more serious. His mother corrected him, but said that she would not hug him for a half hour. He went away disappointed.

Soon, the boy returned and said, "Mom, if you asked God to forgive you, I'll bet He wouldn't say 'wait a while.'"

He got his hug.

Forgiveness is a powerful thing.

As the Lord has forgiven you, so you also must forgive. (Colossians 3:13)

Holy Spirit, help me give others the benefit of the doubt. Help me be generous in forgiveness.

Comfort from a Cow

Sisters Margaret Roozen and Francette Malecha first took care of foster children at a daycare center in St. Paul, Minnesota. At the time, they had a dog and some zebra finches.

"We would turn and see a child sobbing into the fur of the dog," says Sister Margaret. "The children would always go to the animals for comfort before they'd go to us." So when the Sisters learned that a highway was to be built right through the center, they decided to move their children and animals to a farm.

Since then, more than 40 severely neglected and abused children have stayed with them as have goats, pigs, chickens, a tiny spotted donkey and a tan cow.

Jason first came to stay with the Sisters when he was two. When he grows up, Jason tells Sisters Margaret and Francette, he's going to buy the farm next door so he can take care of them.

Whatever dreams and plans you have, leave room for love.

Train children in the right way, and when old they will not stray. (Proverbs 22:6)

Encourage me to love my neighbor, Savior, as You love me.

Picture the Difference

Catholic Digest magazine asks youngsters from kindergarten through the eighth grade to illustrate, in poster form, how their good deeds and caring affect their world. The magazine makes a contribution in the winner's name to the charity that he or she selects.

Elizabeth Weber's poster showed her and her family visiting elderly parishioners, cleaning up their neighborhood, and working at a soup kitchen. Matthew Sprock's poster showed how his family worked together to donate 523 bales of their own hay to a drought-stricken farm family in Texas.

Andy Greenwood's submission illustrated a few of the service projects he has completed: painting a neighborhood church, collecting books for a local hospital.

Caitlyn Beck's poster showed her helping a younger girl tie her shoelaces.

The world really can become a better place, one child, one adult, at a time.

To love Him...and one's neighbor as oneself—this is much more important than all whole burnt offerings and sacrifices. (Mark 12:33)

This day, Father, may my words and actions help others to see You.

Making Your Life a Mellow-Drama

"Life," teaches stress reduction expert Richard Carlson, "is not an emergency." Carlson, author of *Don't Sweat the Small Stuff...and It's All Small Stuff,* believes that each of us creates a great deal of our own stress – and admitting it is the first step on the path to becoming peaceful.

Yes, sometimes we do have to deal with "big stuff." But in general, it's the "little things" that make us tense. How to relax?

"Just slow down a tiny bit," Carlson offers. "Take an extra minute, take deep breaths." He recommends asking the question, "Even a month from now, will this really matter?"

And, he says, "We run so fast chasing productivity and happiness that we can never catch them. If we'd just stop and turn around, we'd let them catch us."

After all, "the purpose of life," Carlson concludes, "isn't to get it all done, but to enjoy each step along the way."

Whoever loves (Wisdom) loves life. (Sirach 4:12)

Slow me down, Lord of Life, so that I may see You in all things this day.

War, Peace and a Moment in History

Paul Tibbets looks back unapologetically over half a century after piloting the Enola Gay, the plane that dropped the atom bomb on Hiroshima, Japan.

Then Colonel Tibbets was recruited in 1944 to organize and train an Air Force unit that would carry atomic weapons. If the mission were successful, he realized "We might shorten this war. ...I realized the responsibility I was taking on. ...I didn't have time to think about the future consequences."

Tibbets and his crew dropped "Little Boy" over Hiroshima the morning of August 6, 1945. "Some people think I should feel guilt. But I have no regrets. ...What people don't realize is: War is a...dirty thing."

War *is* a dirty thing. That's why we must strive, with God's help, to settle disputes by mediation and reconciliation, not warfare and bloodshed. Make peace a way of life.

They shall beat their swords into plowshares, and their spears into pruning hooks; nation shall not lift up sword against nation, neither shall they learn war any more. (Isaiah 2:4)

Spirit of Peace, guide us towards reconciliation with justice.

What's Up Doc?

The best prescription for good health care is one you and your doctor write together. Consider these suggestions for communicating with your doctor.

- Before your visit jot down anything since your last visit that's health related. Bring along a pencil and paper to take notes.
- Be honest, even if some topics embarrass you. Remember your doctor has heard it all before.
- Ask everything about new prescriptions. If you have any reservations about the new drug, say so.
- If you have an opinion about tests or treatments, speak up!
- Sum up the visit in your own words before leaving the doctor's office. Any confusion about your condition, treatment or medication can be cleared up on the spot.

You have an obligation to care for your health.

(Physicians) pray to the Lord that He grant them success in diagnosis and in healing. (Sirach 38:14)

When I call out to You, Jesus, hear and answer me.

Hurricanes and Other Minor Things

Setting off to cross the Atlantic Ocean, alone, in a 23-foot rowboat is a daunting task, to say the least. In 1998, Tori Murden aimed to be the first woman in history to accomplish this goal. She did not make it. Tori was rescued from a hurricane and went home with a dislocated shoulder.

Tori Murden began rebuilding her salvaged rowboat. "I went back not because I'd failed but because I'd very nearly succeeded. I knew I had it in me. ...It doesn't make any difference to humanity whether a woman has rowed across the Atlantic. But if my rowing helps other people decide to pursue their dreams, so much the better."

She would not give up her dream. The following year Tori Murden succeeded, crossing from the Canary Islands to Guadeloupe in the French West Indies.

Faith and determination can lead to success.

He did not despise or abhor the affliction of the afflicted...but heard when I cried to Him. (Psalm 22:24)

Keep me mindful of Your eternal strength and support, Heavenly Father.

Scrolling through Time

In 1937, Quentin Roosevelt took an interest in scrolls that his father, Theodore, Jr., had brought back from China a decade before. Although more informal, they contained drawings that resembled Egyptian hieroglyphics. Roosevelt and his colleague, Joseph Rock, collected more than 3000 manuscripts which are now at the Library of Congress.

Subsequent research has shown that the scrolls date to the Naxi civilization which began to flourish in the eighth century near what is now the Sino-Tibetan border. Cultural anthropologist Zhu Bao-Tian, who learned the Naxi language when he lived with them in the late 1950s, is translating the scrolls.

The rites detailed in them include everything from prayers for healing and longevity to rituals for romance and love. In an article for *Civilization*, Zhu calls the manuscripts "a living fossil for the study of ancient religion."

Keep your spirituality fresh and alive.

**There is nothing new under the sun.
(Ecclesiastes 1:9)**

Fill us with wonder, Lord, at how deeply we are connected to those who have gone before us.

The Subway Soloist

David Allakhverdov lugs an electric piano into the subway, puts fingers to keys and transforms a crowd of train riders into an audience. He was only 12-years-old and new to New York from Uzbekistan when he first played underground. Now, several years later he is enrolled at the Julliard School's pre-college program.

Allakhverdov, whose doctor father was his first teacher, was rejected when he first auditioned for Julliard. He worked harder than ever, and a year later made it. He's won an honors recital competition, and a spot as a soloist with the Pre-College Symphony.

David Allakhverdov is living his dream and his passion. Talent and hard work make an unbeatable combination for success, no matter the handicaps that must be overcome.

The God of heaven is the one who will give us success. (Nehemiah 2:20)

Help me listen to the music of my heart and Yours, Loving Father.

Mr. Rogers Would be Pleased

According to *Family Circle* magazine, studies show that people who live in close-knit communities are more likely to experience greater satisfaction with their personal lives, better health and even greater economic well-being. "How well do you know the family next door?" author Barbara Bartocci asks.

She then lists 50 different ways to reach out in your neighborhood. Among the suggestions she makes is that new neighbors should not wait for a welcoming committee. She cites one woman who put seed packets in the mailboxes on her street, with a note saying "I hope our relationship will flower." She soon had a host of new acquaintances.

Bartocci reminds readers not to forget about the pleasures of bartering, either. "If you sew and your neighbor pounds a mean nail," she says, "agree to do her minor mending if she will perform minor household repairs for you."

We all have the opportunity to be neighbors, to choose whether or not to be good ones.

Lord, help me. (Matthew 15:25)

Show me ways to relate to others, knowing we will brighten each others' lives, Lord.

Holding onto Hope

The minute Mary Lovato learned she had cancer, she "closed everything off. I couldn't talk," she says. Then 32, the Native American woman was given no more than a year to live.

That was in 1987. She nearly died, but managed to pull through after a bone marrow transplant.

Today, Mary Lovato works to increase awareness among cancer patients about hope and survival. The group she founded, a Gathering of Cancer Support, is now offered in twenty other Native American communities and serves as a model for similar groups nationwide.

Hope is most difficult when most necessary, it seems. How can you help foster hope when life is most challenging?

Hope that is seen is not hope. ...But if we hope for what we do not see, we wait...with patience. (Romans 8:24-25)

Jesus, I pray for the ability to have faith and hope, so that I may best serve You.

Rediscovered – At Age 79

His loyal admirers consider musician Chico O'Farrill the "Duke Ellington of Latin Jazz." Yet, most people have never heard of O'Farrill.

Despite his role in creating the musical genre today known as Latin Jazz, and even the reverence of his peers, including Benny Goodman and Count Basie, O'Farrill has always been the least visible of the Latin Jazz innovators.

After more than 50 years in the business, though, O'Farrill is finally on the brink of fame. Thanks to his regular gig in a New York City club with his 18-piece orchestra, he is garnering the recognition he's always deserved – at age 79.

O'Farrill accepts his career's timing. "Frankly," he says, "things happen when they happen."

Waiting can be hard under the best of circumstances, but sometimes the reward makes the wait all the more worthwhile.

For everything there is a season, and a time for every matter under heaven. (Ecclesiastes 3:1)

God, help me accept that all things come to pass in Your time, not mine.

Can You Imagine?

Am I "normal?" is a deep-seated question to which all of us crave the answer at some time or another. Are my dreams common? Do others face similar struggles with co-workers? Does anyone else find it hard to speak up in the face of injustice?

Novelist and clinical social worker Amy Bloom would say the answer is generally "Yes!" Of course, that applies to other people as well. Bloom writes that people are quick to create a line that separates normal from abnormal. She suggests that it's easy to blame people who do things differently. "We prefer to be anxious, even angry about others' 'abnormality'," she explains, "so we don't have to look at our own complications."

The next time you meet someone who approaches life from a different perspective, let go of your inclination to judge. Instead, challenge yourself to celebrate life's rich diversity. And don't forget to be gentle on yourself, as well.

My beloved is all radiant and ruddy, distinguished among ten thousand. ...altogether desirable. (Song of Solomon 5:10,16)

Help me appreciate Your beauty expressed in so many different ways, Beauty ever ancient, ever new.

Insightful Look into Scripture

Rev. Robert Barron, assistant professor of theology at Mundelein Seminary, Illinois, writes in *U.S. Catholic* some thoughts on the study of Scripture.

Barron says that he studied the Bible from numerous angles as a seminarian: from a literary standpoint, from a historical standpoint, and from the perspective of an editor, "teasing out the theological aims of the author."

While acknowledging the importance of each of these methods, Barron would like to see Scripture study include "contemplation of the Bible in its natural setting of prayer, worship, and soul transformation." Then, "after raising our own questions we should let the Bible question us."

Do you own a Bible? Do you read it daily? In its depths you will find beauty, truth and nourishment.

All Scripture is inspired by God and is useful for teaching, for reproof, for correction, and for training in righteousness, so that everyone who belongs to God may be proficient, equipped for every good work. (2 Timothy 3:16-17)

Bless us with understanding and wisdom, inspired by Your Word, Creator God.

Marvelous Mustard

You may think of it as ordinary, a condiment that enhances the flavor of a hotdog or burger or adds piquancy to a sauce. But in Mount Horeb, Wisconsin, people see mustard as much more.

Mount Horeb is the site of the Mustard Museum. Here, you can learn that because mustard contains virtually no cholesterol it is a condiment that "cuts the mustard" at many a dinner.

There are literally thousands of flavors of mustard: lemon peel, tarragon, ginger and pineapple, to name a few. The museum details the history of mustard, as well as its role in the evolution of the American palate and commerce.

Like mustard, human beings come in many different "flavors." And like mustard they are often the liveliness that makes life exciting for others.

Learn to appreciate the uniqueness of each human person.

The kingdom of God...is like a mustard seed that someone...sowed in the garden; it grew and became a tree. (Luke 13:18,19)

Father God, please help me remember that in Your eyes, I am special, unique, irreplaceable.

For the Fun of It

Preeta Bansal became New York State's Solicitor General by way of India and Lincoln, Nebraska. She was born in India, and spent her childhood in Nebraska. She was only 16 years old when she went to Harvard Law School.

She oversees 40 lawyers and represents New York in state and federal courts.

But the most interesting aspect of this extraordinary woman's success is that although she's regarded as a "legal superstar," Preeta Bansal is notoriously merry, cheerful and personable. She has even "stopped being my own worst critic."

Success doesn't have to mean giving up having fun. Open yourself to the happiness of God's bright presence.

Human success is in the hand of the Lord. (Sirach 10:5)

Jesus, may the joy of Your message be present in my life daily. And may I spread Your joy to others.

Looking below the Surface

When Scott Mitchen stares into Lake Superior, he sees much more than a vast body of water. He sees an unusual type of wood.

Mitchen, in 1989, was the first to discover the well-preserved but forgotten logs on the Lake floor.

What makes the buried wood so special? Due to environmental constraints before they were cut, the trees matured slowly, often over hundreds of years. As a result, the wood grain is more compact and tighter than wood from today's tree-farm trees.

Mitchen's efforts helped shed light on a bit of history, as well as developing marketplace demand for this special wood.

If you look closely enough, you'll see opportunities for change where you may not have expected. Even if it means looking beneath the surface.

Unless you change and become like children, you will never enter the kingdom of heaven. (Matthew 18:3)

Thank You, Father, for all life's joyous discoveries.

The Value of Animals

Archeologists eager to learn more about the early origins and the daily lives of our ancestors sometimes turn to today's animals for clues.

One of the techniques used is the study of the DNA of animals both dead and alive. This yields useful information for the experts who know how to decode it.

Anthropologists curious about human settlement of the Polynesian islands, for example, examine the DNA of South Seas rodents. Because the rats stowed away with early ships' passengers, studying them offers clues about human migration patterns. That is more reliable than testing the DNA of the present-day islanders.

Our domestic pets' DNA also tell scientists something about our past migrations.

This is a reminder that no problem lacks a solution. Look for innovative answers to problems.

Encourage one another. (1 Thessalonians 4:18)

Enable us, Jesus, to remain hopeful in spite of difficult problems.

Please Touch!

Kimberly Ridley felt like a captive as a child. "I wasted a lot of energy trying to be obedient, especially in school," she says. "Stop daydreaming!" "Don't touch!"

Outside, her spirit could soar. "I wanted to feel each small bright thing," she says. "The wooly bear tickling my palm as it curled into a perfect circle, the delicate stems of violets, the forbidden cool of swamp water seeping into my shoes."

Now living with her husband in an untamed area of Maine, Ridley still feels she's only scratched the surface of her love for nature. She can tell a red spruce from a white, recognize sarsaparilla, and identify birds by their songs. "But this is only the beginning," she insists.

If each of us developed a more intimate relationship with nature, we would enhance our comfort with each other and ourselves.

No longer shall they teach one another, or say to each other, "Know the Lord," for they shall all know Me, from the least...to the greatest, says the Lord. (Jeremiah 31:34)

Draw us into deeper communion with Your creation, Lord.

Full Steam Ahead

At 16 feet long and weighing nearly ten tons, the 1920 Huber steam traction engine was regarded by many as an oversized eyesore. Yet this steel monster was responsible for helping turn the buffalo's pasture into America's breadbasket.

The Huber, one of many such engines developed during the 19th and early 20th century, was used where hand or horse-drawn plows were useless to break up rock-solid soil. While the land and climate of the great Plains were ideal for growing grain, harvesting the fields required more than mere elbow grease.

Ungainly, bulky but colorful, the Huber was soon obsolete. Today it stands as a reminder of the courage and toil of our nation's homesteaders.

Consider the ways you benefit from the efforts of men and women who lived decades ago.

Let us now sing the praises of...our ancestors. (Sirach 44:1)

Holy Spirit, please bless the courageous and the hard working men and women who help shape our nation.

Up, Up, and Away

"If you're the type who always sees the glass as half empty, then your negative mood could be affecting more than just your outlook on life," say the editors of *Woman's Day* magazine.

They point to studies suggesting that pessimists are more prone to depression and have poorer overall physical health than optimists.

What to do if you're not used to a rosy outlook? One suggestion is to write down your negative thoughts. According to Adam Khan, author of *Self-Help Stuff That Works,* "writing them down gives you something tangible that you can argue with."

Other ideas are to listen to upbeat music or visit with friends who are positive. Exercise, even a quick walk, is also a mood-enhancer.

In developing any good habit, practice makes perfect.

Hope in the Lord. (Psalm 130:7)

Help me, Lord, appreciate how, despite any difficulties, my life is truly good and plentiful.

Dancing on Air

You might see two dancers performing a duet, buoyed only by the wind; or a group of five dancers flip and twirl in mid-air, then against the vertical wall of a 2,700-foot cliff. Is it a special effects trick in a movie?

No. There are no smoke or mirrors involved in the daring feats of Project Bandaloop, a dance troupe that performed in the Yosemite wilderness with harnesses, ropes, and mountain climbing gear for crowds of amazed spectators.

Once secured with their gear, the dancers push out from the rock and in the few seconds of airborne travel, they move in synchronized grace. While watching the troupe perform, an enthralled viewer said, "I cannot believe it."

Believe it. You can break the boundaries that limit your creativity. You'll feel as though you're walking on air!

Dare to speak the word. (Philippians 1:14)

God, You gave me the ability to create and transform. I pray that I remain open to new ideas always.

A New Prescription for His Career

For Robert Lopatin of New York City, the prescription for a fulfilling no-regrets life is this: Don't be afraid of change and never pass up an opportunity to try something new.

To prove that he takes his own advice to heart, Lopatin completed medical school at age 55. When he began a four-year residency at Montefiore Medical Center in the Bronx, he became one of the oldest first-year residents in the country.

He works 100-hour weeks, including exhausting overnight calls. In addition, he often works alongside colleagues young enough to be his children. None of this seems to faze him. On the contrary, he's thrilled with his choice. "It's like nirvana," laughs Dr. Lopatin. "It's like I died and was born again."

Change can be daunting, but offers the opportunity for fulfillment, satisfaction, and fun. It depends on how you look at it.

The Lord...will not change. (Hebrews 7:21)

Give me the courage to make those changes, Holy Redeemer, that will enrich my life.

Expect the Unexpected

Javier and Lena Andrade had been married for ten years without a child. They turned to God and doctors for help. No stork flew over.

In their eleventh year of marriage they adopted a beautiful baby girl. She immediately became their pride and joy. Life went on blissfully for the new parents until four years later when Lena was diagnosed with a serious ulcer. It was frightening news. Javier and Lena comforted each other, and privately panicked.

Two weeks later, Lena returned to the doctor's office and calmly said, "Doctor, this isn't an ulcer." It was their next child, already more than a month along. Born of God's will, after the couple had stopped wishing and trying, their second daughter came all on her own, after a perfectly healthy pregnancy. The couple's previous doctors were stymied. Their family flourishes today.

Trust God to guide you according to His timetable.

Commit your cause to the Lord; let Him deliver — let Him rescue the one in whom He delights

Bring me back to Your peace and reassurance, my Lord.

Self-Serve Society?

Have "feelings" and "sensitivity" challenged "thinking" in mainstream society?

Essayist John Leo points out in *U.S. News & World Report* that in the popular films "Tarzan" and "Star Wars," the key characters are urged to feel, not think, in order to achieve their goals. Leo writes, "Listening to your heart is important, but Tarzan wouldn't last two days in the jungle if he forgot what he saw and merely consulted his feelings."

Leo says that America has begun leaning toward a feelings-centered morality. The danger of this shift, he believes, is that if the self becomes more important than society, personal, individual values could take precedence over the common social or traditional values that keep our nation unified.

Individuals make up a nation, but we still need common values to enable a nation to endure.

Free citizens will serve a wise servant.
(Sirach 10:25)

God, may the citizens of our great nation never lose sight of the importance of community and shared values.

A Crop of Butter Beans and Courage

When Marion and Jerry West moved into their Lilburn, Georgia, home in the 1970s, Jerry decided to plant a garden. Everything grew well, especially the butter beans.

Then, in the early 1980s, Jerry was diagnosed with inoperable cancer. Marion wondered how she would go on without him. For his part, Jerry continued tending his garden.

One day, Jerry went to pick butter beans and Marion, who had done little in the garden over the years, decided to go with him. Together, they picked and shelled their crop. Often on that fall afternoon, Marion's gaze met her husband's, and the two smiled. Jerry died the following summer. Some of the butter beans they had picked the previous fall were in the freezer. So, too, the memory of that afternoon in the bean patch under the Georgia sun.

Treasure your memories of joy and, especially, love.

His memory is as sweet as honey. (Sirach 49:1)

We praise You, Creator, for You give us all good things.

Friendly Persuasion

Lisa Belzberg is a woman on a mission. Through her many contacts and friends in New York's corporate, financial and entertainment circles she is out to raise the quality of public education in a city where that need is paramount. Her non-profit group, PENCIL (Public Education Needs Civic Involvement in Learning), plays matchmaker between givers and schools.

Five years ago she took over the Principal for a Day program, which puts well known people from different fields inside public schools to expose them to the daily reality.

Belzberg acknowledges problems from budgets to the lack of support from too many parents. But she also believes that her program can help raise quality. "By now we have 5000 people who've said, 'I loved what was going on in my school, and I want to be a part of making those human beings' lives better.'"

How do you use your influence for positive change?

Do what is right and good. (Deuteronomy 6:18)

Holy One, how can I use my abilities and influence for the greater good?

The Love of a Language

During one week in New England's Berkshire hills some 200 people gathered to play baseball, do yoga and tai chi, sing campfire songs, dance, listen to lectures and watch movies. An unremarkable week, except that every word was in Yiddish.

Yiddish is the language of Eastern and Central European Jews. It is written with Hebrew letters but it is mainly Germanic, with some words from Hebrew and Slavic languages. Before World War II, Yiddish was the daily language of millions. Then came the Holocaust. Today, Yiddish is used daily by only about 700,000 people worldwide.

The weeklong "retreat," first run in 1976, draws more and more participants. All who meet each year for *Yiddish-vokh* (Yiddish week) – be they 60 or 16, from New York or Japan – share a common love for a language.

Language is precious. Treat your words with care.

How is it that we hear, each of us, in our own native language...about God's deeds of power? (Acts 2:8,11)

In the quiet of each day, Father, I listen for Your voice.

Lessons from a Seven-Year-Old

After Hurricane Floyd caused the largest evacuation in U.S. history, Drew Humphrey, saw hundreds of homeless kids on television – and he had a question.

"What will those kids play with now?" he asked his mom.

Nothing, his mother told him, saying that the North Carolina children had lost everything in the floodwaters. Drew decided to give them his toys.

His generosity inspired others – and soon a police escort was leading two UPS trucks and a 12-vehicle convoy to where 300 kids waited for a share of 1,000 new toys donated from Drew's home state of West Virginia, as well as from Virginia, North Carolina and Kentucky.

Drew's family even adopted nine flood families, to whom they continue to deliver beds, socks, clothing – and yes, more toys. Drew visited the flood-ravaged areas: "Some people were crying," he said. "I prayed a little bit."

A generous heart knows no age limits.

I will give you my support. (2 Samuel 3:12)

My faith in You is Your greatest gift to me, Lord. Help me to share it with others.

Ouch, That Hurts!

No matter how objective, helpful and tactful, criticism is hard to hear; harder to put to good use. Yet criticism can be a help to improve skills or more fully realize one's potential.

Dawn Hudson, writing in *Office Hours,* suggests these responses to criticism:

Say 'thanks' even if you don't agree. If the feedback is negative, don't defend yourself.

Take time to honestly answer this question: "Was the feedback accurate?"

Ask for the reasons behind the criticism: what needs change and why, with examples. If your critic lacks reasons, the criticism may have been unfounded.

Implement agreed upon changes. Follow through is the first step in putting useful and important feedback to work for you.

Perspective can help you see potential in even the most negative circumstances. Could you have viewed it positively? What good could be derived from it now?

A cheerful heart is a good medicine.
(Proverbs 17:22)

Jesus, help me avoid that negative thinking which erodes my spirit and dampens my enthusiasm for life.

Only on Sunday

"And on the seventh day, God rested."

In the busyness of daily life, it is easy to forget to rest. And because we don't rest, we can lose our way; miss the quiet moments that bring us wisdom; the joy and love born of effortless delight.

Set aside your Sabbath day, and observe one or more of these rituals, to summon the healing, sustaining quiet.

Light Sabbath candles say a prayer or blessing for yourself or loved ones and let the world go.

Make a Sabbath meal to unite family and friends. Decorate the table with flowers and candles.

Take a Sabbath walk, with no specific destination or time in curiosity and silence.

Make time for God everyday of the week.

Refrain from trampling the Sabbath...call the Sabbath a delight...honorable...then you shall take delight in the Lord. (Isaiah 58:13)

In the still of this day, Father, hear my cry to You, help me in my needs.

Crafting the Present

The sun-dappled region of Tuscany, Italy, is home to several artisans whose crafts are likely to disappear with them. The pace and expense of modern life make the arduous process of apprenticeship nearly impossible.

Among the craftspeople are the last four women in the De Martini family who weave silk and velvet damask. According to Lorraine Alexander, who visited the workshop, a bank in Genoa has donated funds to build a workshop where 33-year-old Stefania will teach a new generation. "Does she feel the weight of responsibility for the future of her craft?," Alexander wondered. "I don't look ahead," Stefania De Martini replied.

The answer gave Alexander pause. Reflecting on tradition, she sees the "eternal present structured by a mythic past." Yet, "today's global economy reverses that – an anxious present continuously restructured by an imagined future."

Businesses and people must look ahead. The wisest do so while embracing the lessons of the past.

Remember the days of old, consider the years long past. (Deuteronomy 32:7)

Spirit of Holiness, help me prepare for the future with an appreciation for the past.

The Staff of Life

You will probably eat some form of bread today. A bagel for breakfast, croutons on your salad, a roll with your dinner.

If you're lucky, you may get to indulge, savoring the texture and smell of bread fresh from the oven. Whether you're enjoying a flaky croissant, a specialty bread, or the convenience of a peanut butter sandwich, take a moment to offer thanks for the many hands that brought the bread to your table.

Think of the farmers who rose at 4 a.m. to till their fields, plant and nurture the wheat, and get it to market. Think of those who milled the flour, those who baked the bread, and those who delivered it to your local grocery store.

Consider, too, spending a Saturday morning making bread from scratch, immersing yourself in a process thousands of years old, working in solidarity with those dedicated to your well-being every day.

The necessities of life are water, bread, and clothing. (Sirach 29:21)

Thank You, God, for the unseen hands and hearts to whom we are connected in so many ways.

Helping God Move In

It is easy to think of places like cathedrals, shrines or temples as sacred.

But sacred places (and practices) can also exist or be created in our own homes. These gestures, places, words shape us, change us, lift us and our children up. Here are suggestions to help God "move in" with you.

- Create a distraction-free space in your house or apartment. Such a place of relative quiet can indeed be sacred.
- Put pictures of family and friends, relatives' prayer cards, a motto, a favorite family prayer on your refrigerator door.
- Broaden the sense of "family" by learning about other cultures and countries, helping your children see our connectedness as one family of God.

Delve into your religious tradition and learn about others. Encourage the spiritual growth of family and friends.

Has not one God created us? (Malachi 2:10)

Father, we are all Your children. Help us to see You in those we meet this day.

Life Schematics

Since the tender age of five, building conservator William Stivale has been trained to understand what makes a building work. He learned how to appreciate the inherent characteristics of natural materials. "Wood and stone need to breathe, almost like living things," he notes.

Stivale has devoted much of his career to educating and working with mostly volunteer building committees at places of worship. He always insists on taking the entire building into consideration when approaching restoration projects.

"The most useful service I provide is a master plan," he says. "I tell church committees, 'Let's look at the next 5, 7, and 10 years and decide what you have to do now to avoid further problems'." He likens his holistic approach to preventative medicine.

Most of us would be well-advised to apply Stivale's approach in our lives. When did you last review the master plan for your life?

The plans of the diligent lead surely to abundance. (Proverbs 21:5)

Stop the noise, Lord, and help me focus on the big picture.

Building Real Self-Esteem

"Self-esteem has become the single most important consideration in child-rearing and education," says Marshall Duke, a professor of psychology at Emory University in Atlanta.

The trouble is, the idea that a child who has plenty of self-esteem will be both a high-achiever and popular is not the case. Self-esteem can help a child deal with tough situations and failure. But it cannot simply be given, it must be earned. How? Youngsters should set out to achieve a difficult goal and either reach it or believe that they have made the best effort they can.

Praise is actually most meaningful when a parent or other adult does not try to impose adult standards and leaves room for greater accomplishment. Children appreciate the truth.

All of us need to feel that we are innately valuable, even if we have not done anything special. Saying "I love you" might be the best thing you can do.

Thus says the Lord...I have loved you with an everlasting love. (Jeremiah 31:2,3)

Remind me that You treasure me, Spirit of God.

Children and Friendships

Adults sometimes overlook the fact that friendships are as important to children as they are to adults. Human beings are social animals who depend on and learn from other people. It is the job of parents and mentors to encourage and guide children as they make friends.

Pediatrician Dr. T. Berry Brazelton points out that friendships create a secure self-image and help children understand themselves. They react to others and learn how to get others to react to them. They learn the rules and limits of social interaction.

Children also learn how to play with and care for others. They cultivate a sense of humor through teasing, joking and playing together. And they develop means of coping when relationships break down.

Friendship becomes increasingly important as children meet the demands of society and school as well as peer pressure. A parent's job is to allow children to learn their own way of coping while setting limits and providing safety and security.

Faithful friends are a sturdy shelter...a treasure... beyond price...life-saving medicine. (Sirach 6:14,15,16)

Father, help parents be there for their children and their children's friends.

Birds' Second Chance

Brownsville, Texas is a bustling urban center located along the Rio Grande River. It has established a reputation as a tourist gateway to Mexico.

Brownsville has also attracted more than 160 pairs of exotic parrots, usually found hundreds of miles further south. Experts believe some of the red-crowned and yellow-headed birds escaped from illegal smugglers. Others likely migrated north from Mexico to forage for food after a devastating freeze in 1982.

Unfortunately, the fact that the birds weren't native to the area left them unprotected. Enter Steve Walker of the University of Texas at Brownsville. He and other wildlife enthusiasts worked with the Texas Birding Association to have the parrots designated as native in 1998, thereby protecting the species.

Today the parrots, who mate for life and live as long as 70 years, are thriving among the palm trees of Brownsville.

Enjoy God's beauty and protect it.

God created...every winged bird of every kind. And God saw that it was good. God blessed them, saying, '...let birds multiply on the earth'." (Genesis 1:21-22)

Help us reach out to the weakest among us, O God.

Easy Does It

Patrice Karst admits that as a single mother, she's had her share of rough times. In her book, *God Made Easy,* she mentions ten paths to inner peace which she says will make one's life richer. They are:

- Make God your friend
- Go easy, tread lightly, laugh often
- Choose good company
- Never call a miracle a coincidence
- Dream a little dream
- Pay attention to life's lessons
- Surrender to the flow
- Play
- See the big picture
- Never forget how loved you are

Might some of Karst's suggestions help you find your path to inner peace? Or do you have your own? What's important is to work for inner peace.

Peace be with you. (John 20:19)

You are my priority, Lord. Show me all the little ways I can express this truth.

Management from the Heart

More women than ever are breaking new ground in the workplace, especially as executives. But some of our forbears thoroughly understood the demands of corporate responsibility.

Miss Sarah Reed, for instance. In 1871, in response to the hardships wrought by the Civil War, she was one of thirty women who began "A Home for the Friendless." These women secured a house where they took in orphans. They maintained and furnished the home, secured food, hired staff, and raised funds. Profits from lectures, excursions, theatrical productions and food sold at the state fair added to their treasury.

Staff was hired along the way, but for more than 80 years the orphanage needed no executive manager. Miss Reed was among those who made this possible. Of her 61 years on the board, she was president for 45 years.

Discover your own abilities. Then use them for good.

Give her a share in the fruit of her hands, and let her works praise her in the city gates. (Proverbs 31:31)

Give us peace, Lord, in the knowledge that You will open all doors necessary for us to accomplish Your will.

Who's Helping Whom?

Many churches have a service requirement for those preparing for Confirmation. This gives the candidates a tangible way to express the faith they intend to incorporate into their lives.

Students volunteer for 15 to 25 hours at a non-profit organization. In West Babylon, New York, for example, four students signed on as "puppy walkers" for the Guide Dog Foundation. They became surrogate puppy owner/trainers for several months. While the students trained with the dogs, they went through exercises with their eyes closed. That gave them a taste of what it's like to live as a blind person.

In the end, the service requirement accomplished its goal. Said one student: "I will be sad when the dog goes, but if I help someone, it's worth it."

By word and especially by example encourage young people to lead lives of service.

You shall not revile the deaf or put a stumbling block before the blind...I am the Lord. (Leviticus 19:14)

Show us creative ways, Father of All, to reach out to those in need. Make us willing to go the extra mile.

Learning to Bounce Back

Setbacks, disappointments, sad times are part of life. How do people "bounce back?" According to the chair of the psychology department at Ursinus College, Catherine Chambliss, Ph.D., here is how one can recover from setbacks.

Avoid catastrophic thinking and treat your situation as a challenge not a disaster.

Remember, bad things don't happen because you're bad or unworthy. Be responsible for your part, if appropriate; then focus on what you can change next time.

Learn to laugh off events that are *not* earth shattering or life threatening. In a year or less, they will seem much less significant.

Rely on God's ever present Loving Presence.

The Lord is the stronghold of my life ... Though an army encamp against me ... though war rise up against me, yet I will be confident. ...He will hide me in His shelter in the day of trouble. (Psalm 27:1, 3, 5)

God, my protector, help me keep what's important in perspective.

Kind Words

Prakish Shesadri moved from Calcutta, India to the United States only three months before he boarded his first school bus.

Despite perfect textbook English, he found himself lost in the sea of colloquialisms around him. "That's cool, Man!" "Check it out!" "Yo, sit on it!" By the time the bus arrived at school, Prakish felt like a foreigner again.

"The words that brought back my confidence," Prakish now says, "were 'Hello', 'Good Morning', and 'Help' as in 'May I help you?' That's what my first friend here said the moment she saw me staring around, all confused."

Kendra Kryszkiewicz had immigrated to the U.S. three years before Prakish's family. She understood his confused look and the gaps in his English. Kendra's welcome laid the foundation for Prakish's assimilation. Today he is a successful pediatrician and proud U. S. citizen.

Look around. There is someone hoping you will say, "May I help you?"

Whoever welcomes you welcomes Me. (Matthew 10:40)

Keep me aware, Creator, of all those who want to be welcomed.

Common Decency and Common Sense

She was honored by the United Nations and received the President's Citizen's Medal as well as three hundred other awards. She carried the Olympic torch, and even flicked the switch that dropped the ball in New York's Times Square for the New Year's Eve celebration.

Who was this woman and what did she do? She was Oseola McCarty, an elderly washerwoman from Hattiesburg, Mississippi. For years, she took in laundry and ironing and while only charging people a few dollars was able to amass over $150,000. At the age of 87 she gave it all to The University of Southern Mississippi to endow a scholarship fund for poor students, "so that the children won't have to work so hard."

Yet it was not solely this philanthropic largesse that gained her such celebrity, but her compassionate wisdom. The New York Times called it "a mix of common decency and common sense."

Ms. McCarty once said, "If you want to feel proud of yourself, you've got to do things you can be proud of." Amen.

It is well with those who deal generously. (Psalm 112:5)

Yahweh, bless me with common decency and common sense.

God and Breakfast

The hurry-up attitude of big cities can harden people, but, there are still Christophers ("Christ-bearers") on every block.

A young businessman was buying his breakfast from a street vendor in the heart of town. While he waited, a homeless man asked him for something to eat. In a rush to return to his office, the young man hurriedly ordered an extra cup of coffee and a donut to give to him.

When the vendor totaled up the bill, he charged the customer only for his own order. He said, "You don't have to pay for the rest." The coffee and donut would be "on him". This small act of generosity made an impression on the young man.

The potential for human kindness is universal. Even in cities that pride themselves on being busy with so-called "important" things, there are people doing truly vital, humane things each moment. Taking care of each other is God's will; loving one another without judgment is our goal.

See what love the Father has given us, that we should be called children of God. (John 3:1)

Help us to be good to one another, Creator.

The Spirit in the Ordinary

In the course of ordinary life, it's easy to lose sight of the spiritual. Yet the Spirit is there in ordinary things and ordinary people no matter how commonplace and familiar they may seem.

Given our stressed-out lives, we seek peace and quiet in the predictable. But sometimes, exhilarating, confusing, exhausting, spiritual growth can only be found in the fractious and frustrating events that the ordinary presents to us.

Look at where you live, at the familiar sights and sounds. It's all very ordinary, a place like any other. God is there. We just need to be aware of God's Spirit reflected in all the ordinariness around us.

We are God's own, despite our scruffiness and selfishness. We simply need to recognize His presence in our life.

**Those who...seek Him will find favor.
(Sirach 32:14)**

I recognize that You, Father, see the beauty in all of us and everything.

Perfectly Imperfect

These days it's called New Paltz, New York, and it's a Hudson River Valley college town.

Back in the 1700's this area was settled by French Protestants or Huguenots. They used local clay, sand and stone to build houses with "deeply furrowed roof lines and heavily timbered ceilings" that still stand today on Huguenot Street.

According to Morrison Heckscher of The Metropolitan Museum of Arts, Huguenot Street is a National Historic Landmark and the oldest street in America with original houses, including "a whole village of virtually undisturbed pre-revolutionary 18th century dwellings."

But crumbling chimneys were a particular challenge since it was hard to replicate the historic bricks. Volunteers were recruited to craft "perfectly imperfect" hand-wedged thins (bricks) which reflect the individuality of each brick maker. When they've dried, the thins will be used to repair the chimneys.

As in life, there are times when the imperfect is perfectly fine.

Do not judge by appearances, but judge with right judgment. (John 7:24)

Creator, help us value one another, warts and all!

Resting in Peace

Before the first grave was dug at Mount Auburn Cemetery in Cambridge, Massachusetts, in the summer of 1832, the Boston area faced a crisis. Mausoleums in aged colonial cemeteries were known to split open suddenly, spilling out their long-dead occupants and shocking passersby.

Mount Auburn was built and designed to solve a problem and as a complete departure from those old burial grounds. Gone were the simple slate headstones traditional since the days of the Puritans. Instead, dead Harvard professors lie beneath Roman obelisks; textile magnates, inside pharaonic tombs. Among Mount Auburn's more famous "guests": Henry Wadsworth Longfellow, Oliver Wendell Holmes and Mary Baker Eddy.

Historians credit this cemetery with inspiring countless suburban cemeteries across America, as well as, indirectly, urban parks such as New York City's Central Park. But for those interred at Mount Auburn, including the 650 or so buried each year, it is a final home, a place to rest, in peace.

Seek God's peace in time and eternity.

This perishable body must put on imperishability, and this mortal body must put on immortality. (1 Corinthians 15:53)

Grant us Your peace, Holy Trinity, in this life and the next.

A Reading Rainbow

Actor LeVar Burton became an overnight success story after his role as Kunte Kinte in the miniseries *Roots*. He is also well known as Geordi La Forge on television's *Star Trek: The Next Generation*. But to millions of children he is the book-loving host of PBS' *Reading Rainbow*, a program designed to help young people appreciate the joys of reading.

LeVar Burton calls literacy "one of the fundamental building blocks of self-esteem. If you increase the level of literacy in society, you increase the potential for change, growth and understanding."

His crusade for literacy has obviously been well received. *Reading Rainbow* has garnered 13 Emmy Awards. The key to this success? According to LeVar Burton, "It was a place where I could put my passion."

If possible, incorporate your own passion or interests into your work. You'll love what you do and in turn, will do it well. This recipe for success will bring you your own rainbows.

We beseech You, give us success!
(Psalm 118:25)

Yahweh, may my heart be in all that I do.

Answering a Call to Service

When Kay Shank, a registered nurse at St. Francis Medical Center, Peoria, Illinois, saw an ad for volunteers for a medical mission to Haiti, she asked, "Is this what You want, God?"

Despite her anxiety about traveling alone to a desolate place 100 miles from Port-au-Prince, Shank, after much prayer and discussion, decided to volunteer. She knew that providing health care in Haiti would be a challenge. In addition to the high incidence of AIDS and TB, Haiti still has to combat malaria, dengue fever, scabies, and malnutrition, among other problems.

Yet, what Kay Shank remembers best is the beauty of the people, the fulfillment she received, and a phrase that became a by-word, "You do your part, I'll do mine."

Your involvement in the lives of neighbors is irreplaceable.

Just as you did it to one of the least of these who are members of My family, you did it to Me. (Matthew 25:40)

I pray that I may have the courage to contribute when and where I'm needed most, Lord.

Bicycling to Overcome Cancer

Doctor and amateur cyclist, Jeffrey Murray is in awe of the journey Lance Armstrong has made from cancer patient to Tour de France champion. "We'll never see another story like this in our lifetime," the pediatric oncologist insists.

Armstrong says cancer survivors have to deal "with the disease and its effects. We have a choice as to how we address the rest of our lives."

While completing treatment for stage three testicular cancer Armstrong began the Lance Armstrong Foundation. He and Dr. Murray want to help cancer patients be survivors, not victims. Says Armstrong, "We hope to remove some of the fear and panic from those just diagnosed."

Fear can hurt us in so many ways. Do your best to confront your fears and turn terrors into triumph.

Lead lives worthy of the Lord. (Colossians 1:10)

Spirit of Counsel, guide me in making positive, caring choices.

Friendly Donors

It was just another day for Marco Mattei. He asked Staten Island (N.Y.) District Attorney William Murphy if Murphy needed anything. The D.A. needed a new kidney, and Mattei, his Chief of Investigations, gave it to him.

Not that Murphy asked Mattei to donate an organ, mind you. Mattei just thought it was the right thing to do. However, Murphy's body rejected the kidney, so he had to receive a second donation. This one came from yet another staff member, Detective Daniel Ingellis, his bodyguard and driver.

Murphy remains awed by his staff's generosity. "I'm the beneficiary of some wonderful people," he says. "They never expected anything, and they never asked for anything."

What an example of selfless friendship and giving! May each of us be there for a friend in need when that need arises.

Faithful friends are life-saving. (Sirach 6:16)

Giving freely is the ultimate manifestation of Your love, Lord Jesus.

The Power of Many

In 1994, the Nickelodeon channel began a campaign called "The Big Help" to increase the number of viewers and advertisers.

More than a publicity stunt, this was Nickelodeon's answer to requests from kids world wide who wanted to know how they could help people, animals and the environment.

The channel came up with a volunteer-hours telethon and took time-pledges from millions of young people. Each youngster was responsible for acting on his or her pledge. They painted homes, babysat, collected plastic bottles, cleaned parks and made countless other efforts to better their communities.

"The Big Help" has become an annual event and 28.5 million kids have given over 260 million volunteer hours to their families and communities.

Do not forget your own good intentions – and act on them.

The earth is the Lord's and all that is in it, the world, and those who live in it; for He founded it...and established it. (Psalm 24:1-2)

Remind me, Beloved King, to celebrate Your blessings.

Answered Prayers

Acts of kindness are oftentimes answers to prayers.

Betty Harmon of Akron, Ohio, suffered severe foot and ankle injuries in an accident, and had meager means to pay her bills. Her legs ached as she walked. She prayed for a car as well as a cheaper house.

When she saw an ad for Michelle and Mike Elliot's house, Betty Harmon went to look at it. While it did not meet her needs, she learned that Michelle's '88 Chevy Spectrum was for sale. Harmon was nervous asking the price, but Michelle handed her the keys. "Here, I want you to have it."

The Elliots had immediately recognized Harmon's indomitable spirit and her need. They simply treated her the way they would like to be treated. "The Elliots gave me back my independence," Harmon says. "God answered my prayers through them."

Respond with kindness and generosity. You never know whose prayers you're answering.

Those who are generous are blessed. (Proverbs 22:9)

Help me commit myself to acting selflessly, kindly Spirit.

Changing a Life

Felicia Mercadante knew something about cancer. She had volunteered at a children's cancer camp for 11 years. And her best friend, Jessica, had had a successful bone marrow transplant. Then Mercadante saw on TV that two teens were trying to raise money for a marrow transplant.

Mercadante called Jessica's mother to ask her to help organize a marrow drive. She also decided to be tissue-typed as a potential donor. Within two months, she had raised $8700 to help pay the cost of testing potential donors. Hundreds of people in and around her Pennsylvania town responded to her plea for donors. "Our community came together to do a wonderful thing," Felicia Mercadante exclaimed.

Last year, she started working for the Marrow Foundation in Washington, D.C. "There are lots of things we can't change," she says. "But becoming a donor is an action we can take that could alter an outcome."

By changing her life, one woman has made an immeasurable difference in the lives of others. Do all you can, too.

Excel in all that you do. (Sirach 33:23)

Inspire me to make changes for the better, Lord.

Blessed Are They Who Have Not Seen

The search for Noah's Ark has captured the imagination of scientists and seekers throughout history.

Former astronaut James Irwin is among those who have scaled the summit of Mount Ararat in Turkey more than once, looking for evidence of the ark's existence.

Few stories in the Bible are more intriguing than that of Noah, a righteous man and his family. With or without proof, many believe with Carol Meyers, professor of biblical studies and archeology at Duke University, that "the story of Noah teaches that the universe in which we live is moral and that God punishes immorality."

People will continue to search for Noah's physical ark. But time and energy spent on locating the inner ark where the Holy One dwells is far more important. Spend some time reading the Bible and on nourishing your soul.

'Rabbi where are You staying?'...'Come and see.' (John 1:38,39)

Guide my journey to Your dwelling place within me, Jesus.

Exploring the Education Galaxy

When George Lucas refers to Edutopia, he's not talking about some planet in a galaxy far, far away but his goal for an ideal educational system. "It's a shame," he says, "when young people don't like going to school and aren't engaged by the experience."

In Edutopia, students, with the support of dedicated teachers and involved members of the community, would use the most recent technologies to work together on special projects. "Edutopia is what we think learning looks like at its best." To further his goal, he has set up a foundation which collects educational success stories and spreads information via the media: films, CD-ROMs, the internet and books.

Lucas, who was once a bored daydreamer in school–an uninspired student–is aiming high. As Lucas says, "Success is knowing people are learning from and sharing this information. It's a struggle sometimes, but we're committed to it."

What commitment to a better future have you made?

**Give success to your servant today.
(Nehemiah 1:11)**

May we teach our children well, Dear Lord.

Beguiling Artistry

The ordinary and familiar things of life interested that extraordinary French master painter Jean-Simeon Chardin who lived from 1699 to 1779.

Included in his beautiful still life *The Attributes of the Arts and Their Rewards,* are books, coins, a pitcher, a palette and paint brushes.

In *Smithsonian* magazine, Phyllis Tuchman writes that the painter portrayed children with tenderness and "caressed color onto the contours of fruits."

She adds, "he ignored frivolity and intrigue, depicting instead the simplicity of everyday life. In his works, common objects and scenes are rendered with dignity...the humdrum becomes beguiling."

If we look carefully we, too, will see the beauty around us. More than that, we can take the time to thank God for the splendor of simple things.

One thing I asked of the Lord, that will I seek after: ...to behold the beauty of the Lord. (Psalm 27:4)

Help us appreciate the beautiful world You have given us, Beautiful Savior.

Not Another Statistic

Years ago, a highly active child had "ants in his pants." Today, he or she is often diagnosed with one of a number of illnesses that may indicate the use of prescription drugs.

For Debra Jones of Oklahoma, this was unacceptable. It had been suggested that her 7-year-old son take the drug Ritalin for Attention Deficit Disorder. In their effort to make symptoms less troublesome, doctors and educators overlooked several non-medical potential solutions.

When her son improved in 1995 without the aid of drugs, Debra Jones founded Parents Against Ritalin to educate people about alternatives to drug therapy for attention disorders. The group believes that "There are some children for whom Ritalin may be the best option. However, there are countless others that are being drugged unnecessarily."

Different people often need different solutions to problems. What's right for one may be totally wrong for another. Inform yourself and talk to others, including experts or professionals. In any serious matter, think things through carefully before choosing.

Be brave. (Sirach 19:10)

Guide me to my path, Father; show me how I may serve.

A Place of Fools?

"Gotham," the word first applied to New York City by writer Washington Irving in 1807, means "Goats' Town" in Anglo-Saxon. It comes from a village near Sherwood Forest in the English county of Nottinghamshire that was the butt of jokes in the Middle Ages because of its foolish citizens.

In the 1,383-page *Gotham: A History of New York to 1898,* author Mike Wallace introduces the reader to fools in that city's history, as well as to prostitutes and socialites, robber barons and reformers and a few wise people as well. Wallace and co-author Edwin G. Burrows are now at work on Volume II which will bring readers to the present day.

So, what makes New York unique? "Its location, plus seizing the advantages." Wallace says that the port was the "indispensable basic" that eventually turned the city into "the headquarters of an industrial continent."

What are the indispensable basics of your life? Consider what is essential to you and why.

Acquire wisdom for yourselves. (Sirach 51:25)

In all times and places, You are there, Father, leading us and showing us Your love.

A Caring Cut

Barbara Walker's mother needed a haircut. Barbara knew that getting her hair done at a salon would be a treat for her disabled mom, but she also knew that the multi-level area and the loud music at the local shop would be hard on her mother.

One day, Ms. Walker spotted a beauty shop tucked in a corner of an aging strip mall. The shop was named after its owner, Cheryl. She decided to give it a try, and brought her mom there.

Cheryl and her associate took the time to pamper the older woman. They were friendly people who made a special effort to include all the customers in the conversation.

Later, when Barbara's mother was hospitalized or ill, Cheryl telephoned to see how things were going. "Watching my mother blossom with all this attention made me realize what small acts of kindness can mean to each of us," Walker says.

The smallest kindnesses are not so small after all.

Remember to show kindness. (Psalm 109:16)

Smile on me this day, Jesus Christ, as I bring Your light to all I meet.

A Man with a Message

Albert Einstein said of him, "Generations to come...will scarce believe that such a one as this ever walked upon this earth."

Mohandas Gandhi began to work for India's independence from British rule in 1915. The goal was finally reached in 1947 when, after nearly two centuries, British colonial rule in India ended.

It is ironic that Gandhi, who relied on passive resistance to achieve his ends, should have been the victim of violence. He was killed by a fanatic opposed to his religious tolerance. Gandhi's whole life was his message. While his vision for India after independence did not come to fruition, his witness became the model for the world's peace movements.

Gandhi has become, in effect, a citizen of the world. His spirit of determination, courage and peace has endured.

Do not be afraid to rely on God and to work peaceably for justice.

The Lord called me...He made my mouth like a sharp sword, in the shadow of His hand He hid me; He made me a polished arrow. (Isaiah 49:1,2)

Reveal Yourself to me, Master, in the words and witness of others.

The Lama's Words of Advice

The Dalai Lama, spiritual leader of many of the world's Tibetan Buddhists, has offered some suggestions for living that could benefit all people, whatever their faiths.

- Take into account that great love and great achievements involve great risk.
- Follow the three R's: Respect for self. Respect for others. Responsibility for all your actions.
- Remember that not getting what you want is sometimes a wonderful stroke of luck.
- Open your arms to change, but don't let go of your values.
- Share your knowledge. It's a way to achieve immortality.
- Be gentle with the earth.
- Judge your success by what you had to give up in order to get it.

Do you live your own philosophy?

Pay to all what is due them...respect to whom respect is due, honor to whom honor is due. Owe no one anything, except to love one another. (Romans 13:7-8)

Help me to respect the beliefs of others, as well as my own, Lord.

Instruments of His Peace

Alan Paton, the South African writer and opponent of apartheid, wrote that "the Gospel is full of reassurances: You are the salt of the world! You are the light of the world! These words were exciting to those who heard them. ...They were given a new sense of their value as persons. Of these none was greater than Francis of Assisi.

"He might well have prayed: ...*To those who do not know who they are, let me teach them that they are the children of God and can be used as His instruments.*

"There are therefore two things for us to do. The first is never doubt that God can use us if we are willing to be used, no matter what our weaknesses. The second is to see that God can use any other person who is willing to be used, whatever his weaknesses, and if need be, to assure him of this truth."

Never doubt God or His infinite love.

I will not forget you. See, I have inscribed you on the palms of My hands. (Isaiah 49:15-16)

Make me an instrument of Your healing, Lord.

Allergic to People

Are you afraid to do or say something that will embarrass you, or make you feel inferior to others around you? Perhaps you are unable to attend parties, return things to a store, talk to members of the opposite sex, or speak up at business meetings?

Imagine feeling "allergic" to people. If that describes you, you may be suffering from social phobia – a fear of social situations and interactions with others. It affects one in eight Americans. There is help in psychotherapy and medication.

If your life is circumscribed by shyness, it's good to know that help exists. But each person needs to define the severity of that shyness. If the problem is just an occasional bout of jitters, one might just need to learn to live with it.

Just do your best to relax. After all, we are all human, with our individual weaknesses – and strengths.

The Lord is the strength of His people. (Psalm 28:8)

You are my strength, Father. Do not abandon me in my hour of need.

Saving Unwanted Infants

TV reporter Jodi Brooks reported the story of a mother and daughter who drowned the unwed daughter's newborn baby rather than face their friends and neighbors.

Brooks, determined to save other unwanted babies, asked the state not to prosecute mothers who abandoned their babies so long as the infants were surrendered unharmed at a hospital.

She developed, A Secret Safe Place for Newborns, which is thriving at several Mobile, Alabama, hospitals. Based on the success of her program and others, 15 states have signed laws exempting mothers from prosecution if they turn over their infants in good health. Says Brooks, "there had to be another option."

Brooks speaks at junior and senior high schools, telling young women to practice abstinence, go to college, find a husband and have a family. Brooks says she "can sleep at night" because she has given infants and their mothers a second chance.

Those who love God must love their brothers and sisters also. (1 John 4:21)

Help us to protect and nurture young lives, Lord.

Respecting Your Spouse

Respect is integral to the long-term success of marriage and close friendships. And, close friendships make for enduring marriages.

But how show respect? Some basics:

- ...*through what you say.* Talk with your spouse or friend as with everyone else, giving them eye contact and positive feedback. Talking about his or her effect on your decisions is an avenue of respect.

- ...*through what you do.* "Respect" means "the act of noticing with attention." Action-related respect means being interested in what interests your spouse or friend.

- ...*through what you think.* "To respect someone is to value them," says psychologist and counselor Dr. Mark Baker. "That involves a process of understanding and acceptance."

Respect in marriage or in friendship acknowledges God's view that the position of spouse or friend is always one of honor.

I am my beloved's and my beloved is mine. (Song of Solomon 6:3)

I promise to respect and love my spouse, my friends, Father of all.

Just a Waste of Time

You don't have time for everything.

If you can accept that and make conscious choices about what you really want to accomplish, you will be on your way to managing your time. And the best way to make plans? Backwards.

Productivity consultant Jan Jasper says that most people either do not plan at all or start at the beginning of the day. And that, she believes, is the wrong way.

"Effective planning works the opposite way," says the consultant. "What you want to accomplish by the end of the year determines what you should do today and tomorrow. Schedule these tasks into your calendar working backward from your goal."

What are your goals? What do you want to achieve at work, with your home and personal life? Think about what you would like your life to be like one year or ten years from now. Do something today to help get you there.

Lead a quiet and peaceable life. (1 Timothy 2:2)

Eternal Trinity, help me create a life in Your image.

Once upon a Story

Bombarded as the modern family is by video games and television, it is easy to forget the simple joys of story telling.

You can grow closer to your children and stoke a curiosity in the world around them that will last a lifetime.

Marshall Shelley, an editor at *Christian Parenting Today* and father of five children, makes these points for tyro storytellers.

- Relate the story to something just seen or heard. Your child sees trees. Peter Rabbit lived in the base of a tree.

- Use your imagination to make where, what, and who questions into vivid images.

- If your child contributes a detail, weave that into the story. Then ask, "What do you think happened next?"

- Finish the story with a positive resolution.

- Encourage your child's questions.

Rewards will follow.

They told the whole story. (Matthew 8:33)

Inspire story tellers, Holy Spirit.

The Discipline of Happiness

What's wrong with being happy?

Some people seem to think that a person happy with their lot is childishly naïve or in denial. But writer Annette LaPlaca says that happiness isn't a natural state, it's a discipline that gets easier through faithful practice.

Gratitude is one key. Of her husband, she writes, "I'm thankful for the hundreds of times David's scrubbed the pots after dinner, for the times he's instantly forgiven my crabbiness...As I think about the multitude of actions that prove David's love for me over the years, I'm filled with joy."

Annette LaPlaca knows that things could be different, and that her husband did not come with a lifetime guarantee when she married him. No one or no thing does.

It is a conscious search for the positive, instead of the negative, that can help bring true happiness.

Happy are those...(whose) delight is in the law of the Lord. (Psalm 1:1)

Be the source and guarantor of my happiness, Jesus.

"Excuse Me"

We all make excuses at times, some more lame than others. According to Craig Boldman and Pete Matthews, authors of *Every Excuse in the Book: 714 Ways to Say "It's Not My Fault!,* there's no mistake that can't be disavowed, dismissed, rejected, shifted, sidestepped, or redirected. Here are a few of their favorites:

"My alarm didn't go off."

"French fries are vegetables."

"I don't know why; I just did it."

"He made me do it."

"There was no warning label."

"Normie's mom let him do it."

"Grandpa ate greasy bacon every morning and he lived to be 103."

Relate to some of these? Well, we all err. And we all have our favorite excuses. Honestly, though, honesty is usually the better policy.

My honesty will answer for me. (Genesis 30:33)

I will not let excuses get in the way of living my life, Generous Giver.

Chipping Away at the Status Quo

In the Capitol Building in Washington, D.C., stands a statue of President Abraham Lincoln. As writer Kathryn Jacob notes in *Smithsonian* magazine, "Few commissions for sculpture had been awarded by the federal government," but in 1866, Congress offered $10,000 for a full-length likeness of the slain president.

Most assumed the plum assignment would go to an established sculptor with many prominent pieces to his name. Nineteen-year-old Miss Vinnie Ream of Wisconsin thought otherwise. Two years earlier, her potential recognized, she had been accepted as an apprentice in the studio of noted artist Clark Mills. Congressmen and politicians who had posed for Ream supported her campaign to secure the commission.

Against all odds, secure it she did, and in 1871, her marble statue of Lincoln was unveiled to great applause.

Do you put limits on your use of your God-given talents?

Each of us was given grace according to the measure of Christ's gift. (Ephesians 4:11)

Lord, do not let me limit anyone, including myself, with preconceived notions.

Soul Friendship

True friendship transforms us. It can sweep away feelings of anonymity and show us the rewards of intimacy.

According to writer John O'Donohue, the ancient Celts had a particularly beautiful concept of friendship known as *anam cara*, Gaelic for "soul friend."

This spiritual guide "was the person to whom one confessed, revealed confidential aspects of one's life." There was a special intimacy between you and your *anam cara*, "an act of primal recognition: allowing your soul friend to "see you from an eternal perspective."

Within these relationships, people were encouraged to be as they truly were, without pretense. And the friendship became a doorway to the eternal. As O'Donohue phrases it, "a friend helps you to glimpse who you really are and what you are doing here."

Our friends can make us better people if we love and support them and let them return the favor.

Wine and music gladden the heart, but the love of friends is better than either. (Sirach 40:20)

Holy Spirit, inspire us to cultivate friendships.

Common Decency

Decency does not seem to be a topic much discussed these days. Perhaps some think it old-fashioned or irrelevant. It's not.

An article from the *Royal Bank (of Canada) Letter* says, "There may be ordinances to ensure decency as it pertains to modesty and morality, but there are none that say that a man or woman can be prosecuted for not treating his or her neighbors with fairness, compassion and consideration. …In a truly well-ordered society, the unwritten law of decent conduct is most strictly obeyed.

Whether obeyed or not decency "makes all the difference to the quality of life in a time or place—and to life itself, for that matter. For "the thin precarious crust of decency is all that separates any civilization, however impressive, from the hells of anarchy, of systematic tyranny that lie in wait beneath the surface," as the superb 20th century novelist and essayist Aldous Huxley wrote.

Make common decency a common part of your life.

Love your neighbor as yourself. (Galatians 5:14)

Just God, help me develop a keen sense of all that is good and right.

Character Counts

To help kids learn about the difference between right and wrong, the late Congresswoman Barbara Jordan, actor Tom Selleck and others founded "Character Counts!" They were motivated by the simple reasoning that "it's difficult for kids to do the right thing when they don't know what the right thing is."

This non-profit, non-partisan education program offers resources like workbooks, videos, and multi-day training sessions. The rights and wrongs they teach are based on what they refer to as the 6 Pillars of Character. They are: trustworthiness, respect, responsibility, fairness, caring, and citizenship.

Members of the organization believe that by embracing these words, all people, not just kids, can make the world a better place. Says one, "If we want to improve the character of our children, we have to improve the character of our communities."

Community begins with one person and so does change. Think about your community and your character and how to improve both.

Cease to do evil, learn to do good; seek justice. (Isaiah 1:17)

Jesus, let my character reflect Yours.

The Man Who Coined "Workaholic"

Dr. Wayne E. Oates, was responsible for the term "workaholic" entering the American cultural lexicon.

In *Confessions of a Workaholic: The Facts About Work Addiction* Dr. Oates wrote that work can be as addictive as alcoholism. He said that the work addict "drops out of the human community: in a drive for peak performance.

Dr. Oates's interest in the subject apparently reflected his own personality. He served in several academic and pastoral posts. And he combined Christian theology with psychiatric insights in order to improve the ability of pastors to counsel people.

Today, unfortunately, being a workaholic has become a badge of honor for too many.

There's nothing wrong with hard work, of course. Beware, though, of excess and obsession. Guard against the power of work, drink, drugs or any other thing to take over your life.

**O God of my ancestors and Lord of mercy...give me the wisdom that sits by Your throne...and she will guide me wisely in my actions.
(Wisdom of Solomon 9:1,4,11)**

Lord, help me realize there is a time to work and a time to play.

Of Mollusks and Mentors

The wood-eating mollusk may not speak to the hearts of many, but Dr. Ruth D. Turner spent a good part of her life adding to the scientific community's knowledge of the clam-like crustacean.

Her research, which resulted in over 100 publications on the topic of woodworms, took her around the world. She led scuba diving expeditions, appeared on *National Geographic* television specials, and was named to the Women Divers Hall of Fame. She felt deeply indebted to Dr. William Clench, her mentor at Harvard University. At one point in her career, she asked him how she could return the kindness he'd shown her.

"You can't," he told her. "Just do it for the next generation." She followed his advice. Upon her death, the *New York Times* cited not only her scholarly achievements, but also the beloved reputation she had earned with her students.

When it comes to generosity of spirit, pass it along.

To each is given the manifestation of the Spirit for the common good. (1 Corinthians 12:7)

Let us praise You in every aspect of our work, Creator.

Miles to Go and Promises to Keep

Before being named Secretary of State, General Colin Powell built a reputation as head of America's Promise – The Alliance for Youth.

The organization's mission is to make sure that each child receives five special gifts that have been endorsed as keys to pointing America's youth in the right direction. They include:

- The presence of responsible, caring, loving adults.
- A safe place in which to learn and grow.
- A healthy start.
- Marketable skills.
- The opportunity to give back.

Colin Powell, the former chairman of the Joint Chiefs of Staff, observed that giving youngsters "things" means nothing if we don't give our children what they need to build character and competence. He pointed out, "the need is always present and acute."

Guide the young people in your life.

Train children in the right way and when old, they will not stray. (Proverbs 22:6)

Show me, Lord, where there are hearts in need.

Wisdom and Warning

"When I am an old woman, I shall wear purple with a red hat which doesn't go and doesn't suit me…"

This opening refrain from the poem "Warning" by Jenny Joseph strikes a chord with many mature women. "It is about finding freedom in reaching the age when you don't care what other people think about you," writes Lori Basheda in the *Orange County Register.*

When Sue Ellen Cooper reached that stage, she bought herself a purple dress and a red hat in celebration. Today there are 175 official chapters of the Red Hat Society. They have no rules and no official purpose. The bankers, nurses, professors, and artists in the society have enough other responsibilities. But they do sometimes get together in their purple dresses and red hats, just for the fun of it.

"We've all raised families or volunteered until we're blue in the face," Cooper explains. Now these women of a certain age want to celebrate freedom, acceptance and the joy of living.

Life offers so much to celebrate.

A disciple is not above the teacher. (Luke 6:40)

Beloved God, free my spirit and feed my soul.

Tied With Kindness

Businessman Joe Hecht learned first hand about the kindness and tie-knotting skills of his fellow New Yorkers.

He was walking to work on a blisteringly hot day. Determined to remain cool, he would keep his shirt unbuttoned until he got to the office. Then he realized that his designer tie, which had remained untied and dangling loosely around his neck, had fallen off somewhere.

Without much hope, Hecht decided to retrace his steps on the chance that the tie might have been overlooked and left on the street. It wasn't. Instead, someone found it, hung it on a nearby pole, and carefully tied it into a perfect knot. A stranger had realized its value and counted on the owner's return.

Kindness can surprise us when it is found in out of the way places, unusual times, or under odd circumstances. But it is just as satisfying to show thoughtfulness as it is to receive it. Today is a perfect opportunity to begin.

Show kindness and mercy to one another. (Zechariah 7:9)

Lord, make me an instrument of your kindness today.

Destined to Fly

The first women aviators taxied down the runway just five years after the Wright Brothers' 1903 flight. Yet women pilots faced social, economic and legal barriers.

In fact, only in the last 30 years have professional training and career opportunities for women pilots become widely available.

That has meant that Dorothy Aiksnoras-Vallee could become a first officer for Northwest Airlines. Evie Washington is a cadet flight orientation pilot for the civil Air Patrol. Patricia Jenkins, a "flying cowboy" uses her plane to herd cattle on her family's Oregon ranch. And astronaut Shannon Lucid was a mission specialist on five space shuttle flights.

When people are denied opportunities, everybody loses. Ask yourself how you can contribute to equal opportunity and justice not just for women and girls, but for all. Then act.

Deborah, a prophetess, wife of Lappidoth, was judging Israel. (Judges 4:4)

Jesus, teach me to be more like You; how to live for others.

Top Cop

In October 1996, Chicago police officer Jim Mullen was shot in the line of duty. The injuries left this young husband and father paralyzed for life.

But instead of going on disability, Jim Mullen opted to remain a cop. He now works as an outreach coordinator for Chicago's community policing program. The job combines deskwork with speaking engagements at schools, houses of worship and community centers.

Despite his reliance on a ventilator and 24 hour nursing care, the always-smiling Officer Mullen says, "This is the hand I was dealt and I just have to play it."

The hand that we're dealt may not always seem like a winner, but the fact is God does not create losers. Our approach to problems can be the most important factor in successfully resolving them. Whatever your troubles may be, pray for the courage to move forward and let God guide your way. Then success will already be yours.

Lead me in Your truth, and teach me, for You are the God of my salvation. (Psalm 25:5)

Lord, bless me with courage and wisdom.

Finding Peace in the Simplest of Pleasures

Here's what some people do to find serenity:

"I put on my ice skates…I put my hands behind my back and glide. I hear the click of the blades on the ice, and the rhythm of the skates…at twilight," explains Bostonian Janice Page.

Once a month, San Franciscan Lizbeth Polo puts on her "favorite terry-cloth bathrobe," listens to soothing music and lights a scented candle.

Sue Kirby, of Portland, Oregon, resorts to humor. She "brought two huge doughnuts to (her) gym class and used them as arm weights. The laughter was contagious," she says.

Julie Bawden of Orange, California, says she "can't think about anything else if I'm gardening. I hear birds sing, feel a slight breeze…having my hands in soil connects me to the earth."

What's your recipe for peace after a hectic day? Take at least a few minutes daily to refresh your soul, mind and body.

Pursue what makes for peace. (Romans 14:19)

Jesus, please give me peace of soul and spirit.

Parents as Partners

Polly Berends hates the term "parenting."

"It turns parenthood, which is a state of adulthood, into a verb and makes it into something that's done to the child," she writes. "It's as if it's the parent who causes the child to be human." This denies the child's individuality and wholeness and neglects what parenthood means in terms of the parent's growth.

The author of several books including *Whole Child/Whole Parent* and *Gently Lead,* Berends believes that when it comes to introducing children to spirituality, the best a parent can do is to prepare the way for a child's spiritual growth.

She advises that "it is best to look at (children), not as do-it-yourself projects at which we can succeed or fail, but as fellow travelers in a mutual journey of spiritual awakening."

Parents, do you respect your children's individuality? Children, do your respect your parents' individuality?

The wolf shall live with the lamb, the leopard... with the kid, the calf and the lion and the fatling together, and a little child shall lead them. (Isaiah 11:6)

What do the children in my life have to show me about You today, Infant of Bethlehem?

The Amazing Edison

Thomas Edison was an amazing fount of creativity from the phonograph and the electric light bulb to countless patents on other inventions. He is quoted as saying he never did a day's work because it was all fun.

One of his favorite inventions – the electric pen – isn't much known today, but it was the first Edison device to be mass-produced and marketed. It helped transform an obscure inventor into the "Wizard of Menlo Park."

More than a pen, Edison's invention enabled users to turn out exact duplicate copies eliminating a lot of tedious work for office clerks. He promoted his product and sales were good. Eventually, he sold rights to his "Electric Pen and Duplicating Process." Other companies developed it into the first mimeograph. Edison had turned his attention elsewhere.

Not all ideas are winners; not even for a genius such as Edison. But imagination combined with perseverance can work wonders. Nurture your own creativity.

Suffering produces endurance and endurance produces character. (Romans 5:3-4)

Turn our attention to the ways we can be creative, Lord.

Toy World, Toy World

Betty Portenier volunteered for more than two decades at a historical museum in northwestern Pennsylvania. She worked hard to develop an interest in everything from Native American artifacts to Civil War heroes.

A vibrant senior citizen, today she is board president of the Marx Toy Museum in Summit Township.

Portenier knew the idea for the museum was a good one, but she also understood how big an undertaking it would be. She needn't have worried. Former employees of the Marx Toy Factory, which was the largest in the world in its heyday, are clamoring to work with her, sharing their time, their memories, and their personal toy collections.

"Everybody's a kid at heart," she observes.

There's so much to learn, to enjoy. Stay open to knowledge and to sharing with others.

Let the little children come to Me. (Luke 18:16)

Keep my dreams alive, Paraclete, and help me remember that it's never too late.

For the Love of Literature

TVs, CDs, DVDs, computers. With all this, nobody reads anymore. Right? Not really.

But what might be true is that it takes something special to cut through all the "noise" and persuade us that literature has value. It seems the "Bookworm," aka Michael Silverblatt, has the necessary passion to turn people into book-lovers.

Silverblatt's half-hour radio show connects authors (famous and little known) and audiences, many of whom are avid listeners.

The California radio host tells how a punk-look teen recognized his voice while they were on a movie line and spoke to him. The youth had accidentally heard the Bookworm's interview with Alice Walker and became a listener.

Silverblatt always believed that "if the conversations were (done) with real passion and authenticity, then the excitement will attract the listener."

Do you live with passion and authenticity?

(May) the genuineness of your faith...result in praise and glory and honor when Jesus Christ is revealed. (1 Peter 1:7)

Encourage in us a passion for life, Lord.

Life in a Cemetery

In the days before Halloween, a small town cemetery was victimized by vandals. One evening, Harry Paige, passing the cemetery, saw an unusual light.

Writing in *Catholic Digest*, Paige said that it turned out to be a night light in the shape of an angel which was clamped on a tombstone at a child's grave. An old woman crouched there.

"She's my granddaughter Sarah," the woman told Harry. "She died when she was only six." The old woman had been keeping the vigil from sunset until midnight to stop the vandalism. "Her light's been stolen twice," she said. "Sarah was always afraid of the dark."

Concerned for her safety, Harry Paige begged the old woman to go home. "I'll take your watch," he said. Until midnight, he sat there, under the angel light, talking to the little child and praying for her and for her grandmother, too.

Pray for all your brothers and sisters, living and dead.

Let us therefore make every effort to enter that rest. (Hebrews 4:10)

Into the darkness, Father, You sent the Greatest Light to lead us to You, to show us the way.

Courage to Go On

Carolyn Goodman could have let grief run her life, but she didn't. Her son, Andrew, then 20, was one of three civil rights activists murdered by the Ku Klux Klan in the summer of 1964.

Days earlier, when he told her he was going to register voters in Mississippi, her heart sank. But, a civil rights activist herself, Goodman knew that to stop her son would be hypocrisy.

Two years after Andrew's death, Goodman and her husband, Bobby, started the Andrew Goodman Foundation that is involved in a wide range of community activities from improving schools to environmental protection. Goodman remains active on the speaking circuit, lecturing to schools, colleges, synagogues and churches about the civil rights movement.

"My life is with young people," she says. Though she still grieves for her son, she has not let that prevent her from encouraging young people to do what is right in spite of the risks.

Decide when it is necessary to take a risk and take courage.

Fear is nothing but a giving up of the helps that come from reason. (Wisdom of Solomon 17:12)

Give us the courage to defeat bigotry, Holy Spirit.

The Challenge of Simplicity

The great 20th Century artist Jacob Lawrence didn't believe in art movements. Maybe that's because his own style, known for its straightforward simplicity, has been emulated and admired by the scores of artists who followed him.

Being simple was complicated, Lawrence often admitted. Discussing art, he said, "We say 'simplicity' and imply something's easy to accomplish, but this isn't easy. It's a highly refined composition...an intuitiveness, maybe. An emotional authenticity."

Being forthright, direct, authentic in our interaction with others – and especially with ourselves – *is* difficult. As the Shaker hymn says, "tis a gift to be simple, tis a gift to be free, tis a gift to come down where we ought to be." But when we are there we are "in the valley of love and delight."

Simplicity and its accompanying freedom, being "where we ought to be," and authenticity are worth striving after.

For freedom Christ has set us free. Stand firm, therefore, and do not submit again to a yoke of slavery. (Galatians 5:1)

Jesus, walk with me in my efforts to simplify and make honest my relationships with others and with my self.

A Sombrero and a Smile

At two, Hannah seemed suddenly scared by persons in strange costumes. Halloween ghosts and goblins terrified the otherwise fearless child.

"It's the monster!" she would shout at the slightest glimpse of a mask or makeup. On the weekend before Halloween, Hannah's parents took her for dinner at a local Mexican restaurant. They were unaware that the staff, celebrating the holiday, were decked out in costumes, from clowns to ghouls. One particular mask – a hideous, skeleton-like face – frightened Hannah right into her father's lap.

At the table next to the toddler and her family was a couple celebrating the wife's birthday. As they got up to leave, the husband gave Hannah his wife's sombrero, a gift the restaurant gives to customers having a birthday "fiesta."

Hannah's tears dried up. Proudly wearing the hat, she smiled at her newfound friends and at her family – even at the man in the frightening mask.

Kindness had driven away the demons.

Kindness is like a garden of blessings. (Sirach 40:17)

Father, enable me to share the light of my life with all I meet today.

A Winding Path Made Straight

"People must know what they believe and then follow it in their lives," says Marianna Daly. She is a living example.

After studying to be a forest ranger, Daly spent a year with the Jesuit Volunteer Corps. Her experience in southern West Virginia included home visits, involvement with a recreation program, and teaching.

The year was life-changing. Drawn to both rural life and outreach, she returned to school for a medical degree. "It was a privilege to go to medical school, and I asked myself, what am I going to do with this chance I've been given?" she commented.

Now part of a small family practice in Asheville, North Carolina, she is able to build strong patient-doctor relationships, particularly with the elderly. She tries to keep this in mind each day: "every person who walks through this door could be Jesus."

Welcome the Lord into your life through each of His beloved people. He wants no less.

You are the body of Christ and individually members of it. (Corinthians 12:27)

Lord, let me see You in everyone I meet today.

A Cardinal's Reflection

By the time of his death from cancer in 1996, Cardinal Joseph Bernardin of Chicago was recognized by many in his city and beyond as a man of great faith, integrity and courage.

Centering his life in God, he wrote, "I have found again and again that when I stopped resisting, stopped trying to be completely in charge of my life and placed my trust in the Lord, things have gone better for me…

"I wish to affirm and encourage you, as you also search for the Lord in your daily lives and seek to grow in intimacy with him. Do you ever feel misunderstood, lonely, discouraged, wounded, abandoned? Then you need to experience Jesus' love, mercy, compassion, and healing power. He is not far away. He is right there beside you, waiting for you to turn to Him and place yourself in His hands."

Speak with Him now, right there beside you.

'You are my refuge, my portion in the land of the living." Give heed to my cry for I am brought very low. (Psalm 142:5-6)

Jesus, You are always near me. Don't let me forget.

The Noblest Pursuit: Truth

It was 1842, and Julia Smith was preparing for the end of the world. A believer in the apocalyptic prophecies of Baptist preacher William Miller, Smith prepared for the day Miller warned was near. He and his followers believed that the Second Coming of Christ was to happen on the very last day of 1842.

When Miller's prophecy proved false, Smith attributed his error to inadequate translation of the Bible. At age 55 she began to translate the Bible herself. After seven years, she had become the first and only woman to translate the Hebrew and Christian Testaments from the original Hebrew, Aramaic, Greek and Latin.

One person's error led another to seek the truth.

How do you seek the truth? Reading the Bible? Other spiritual literature? Prayer? Meditation? Consider the many ways in which you can enrich your spiritual life.

Sing to Him, sing praises to Him...Let the hearts of those who seek the Lord rejoice. Seek the Lord and His strength; seek His presence continually. (Psalm 105:2,3-4)

God, guide and direct my spiritual growth.

Circus Thrills

Long before we had television and other media to entertain us, there was the circus parade. Folks in communities around the country would eagerly await its dramatic and colorful arrival.

The visual feast included not only the brass bands, strange animals and people in a variety of costumes, but also the parade highlight – huge decorative circus wagons pulled by horses in plumes. Everything was bright, colorful and ornate to attract customers to the show.

One clever float from 1882, in the shape of a shoe and featuring children carved into the sides and top, portrayed the nursery rhyme, "The Old Woman Who Lived in a Shoe." A Ringling Bros. Swan Bandwagon had elaborate carvings reminiscent of the statues and gardens at Versailles.

There is so much to see in life's passing parade and so much we miss. Open your eyes and rejoice in God's gifts.

A joyful heart is life itself. (Sirach 30:22)

Fill us with joy and hope, Savior.

A True Finisher

Zoë Kaplowitz has finished last in every New York City Marathon for 12 years even with a five-hour head start. Still, Kaplowitz keeps running the 26.2-mile journey.

Why does it takes her more than 24 hours to complete the course? Kaplowitz has multiple sclerosis. And it has reduced her to a painful, crutch-aided shuffle. She's also diabetic, so she must stop to test her blood every two miles.

On a normal day, Kaplowitz only needs her left crutch; on marathon day, both. Her best friend, Hester Sutherland, who's completed every NYC Marathon except one, also helps her.

Kaplowitz is a motivational speaker, author, and spokeswoman for the National MS Society. Her mission is to help people rethink the term "winning." "People run marathons every day of their lives in one way or another, and we need to...give ourselves the finishers' medals we deserve," she says.

When you give each day the best you've got, you deserve to give yourself a pat on the back.

Run with perseverance the race that is set before us, looking to Jesus the pioneer and perfecter of our faith. (Hebrews 12:1-2)

Encourage me, Holy Redeemer.

Fun with the Kids

In the hustle and bustle of everyday family life, it's easy to lose sight of the importance of plain old fun. From celebrating chores to frolicking in the rain or snow, here are some suggestions on how to have fun with your kids:

- Don't let the TV take over. Use it as a learning tool, not a time-stealing culprit.
- Sing in the rain, taste the rain, dance in the rain. Freedom in a rainstorm is exhilarating.
- Turn the living room into a camping site. The whole family can create tents and forts.
- Read to your child. Love of books is a gift that lasts a lifetime.
- Let household chores become family fun by turning on music and wearing a costume, pretending you're someone else.

Be creative. Lighten up. Share yourself with your children, for their sakes, and for yours.

I am glad and rejoice. (Philippians 2:17)

Spirit of God, help families play together.

One Child's Courage

The Story of Ruby Bridges, written by psychiatrist and author Robert Coles, is the real-life tale of a courageous 6-year-old girl. Ruby Bridges walked past angry segregationists to become the first African-American child to attend New Orleans' William Frantz Elementary School.

For much of that year, 1960, she sat alone in a classroom, learning reading and math from a first-grade teacher who befriended her. White parents kept their children home rather than have them share a room with a black girl. Her story inspired the book by Dr. Coles, as well as a famous Norman Rockwell painting.

On the 40th anniversary of her contribution to civil rights, Ruby Bridges visited an integrated classroom of first-graders in New York City. "I like to share my story with children," she said. "They are amazed by it." As she finished reading her story to the children, a little boy quietly said, "Thanks for changing the law."

Sadly, prejudices still exist. Consider your own attitudes and what you can do to build bridges of tolerance.

Have we not all one father? Has not one God created us? (Malachi 2:10)

Guide us in improving race-relations, Lord.

Beauty in All Sizes

Baltimore psychologists, Miriam Arenberg and Beth Williams-Plunkett, in an hour-long museum program, "Feast, Famine, and the Female Form," use art to teach teenage girls that beauty comes in all sizes and shapes and that standards of beauty have changed across time and cultures.

The program, according to Williams-Plunkett, aims to help women and girls "question this harmful assumption that they have to be thin to be beautiful." They don't expect one hour to change attitudes, but they feel a beginning will have been made.

So far the twice yearly program has been an eye-opener for pre-teen and teenage girls. One said it, "opened you up to a whole lot of things you wouldn't have thought of before."

Beauty *is* in the eye of the beholder. Each of us is different and unique. Honor the beauty of the human form and spirit.

The glory of youths is their strength.
(Proverbs 20:29)

Creator, we cherish the differences You bestowed on us.

A Few Thin Lines Made a Big Impression

You see them on virtually everything you buy now: soda bottles and cans, containers of non-prescription medicines, magazines, compact discs, you name it.

Those little black vertical lines that are better known as the UPC – Universal Product Code – are now so much a part of our daily lives, that we hardly notice them. Yet, they come from the research on electronic data processing in 1973. The eight members of the team had a goal: make shopping faster and easier for consumers who found checking out the least pleasant shopping experience. But the members and the food manufacturers and supermarkets they represented were also driven by economic realities. They had to improve productivity and profitability.

One team's work affected the way the world buys and sells. Not surprising when we consider the impact a single individual can have on others. Your words, actions and attitudes have a far greater reach than you realize. Use your abilities well.

Do not neglect to do good. (Hebrews 13:16)

Father God, I want to make a difference. Help me focus my efforts to benefit Your people.

Two Sisters Battle Cancer

"Today Show" personality Katie Couric lost her husband, lawyer Jay Monahan, to colon cancer. Two years later her older sister developed pancreatic cancer.

Emily Couric, an author and Virginia state senator, was considering a run for lieutenant governor, but bowed out to deal with her cancer. Inspired by Katie's public campaign for colon cancer awareness, she had already pushed through a bill requiring Virginia insurers to pay for cancer examinations.

A friend commented that both sisters are enormous successes who "have been badly treated by fate."

The fact is, we never know what life has in store for us. Virtually everyone experiences suffering of one kind or another.

One thing is for certain: familial love and support are crucial in times of Job-like trials. So is prayer.

The Lord was my support. (Psalm 18:18)

May I show courage and faith in the face of trials, Savior.

A Symbol Passes On

Symbols, especially those imbued with historical and religious meaning, are important.

Sadly, Annapolis, Maryland had to bid farewell to one of its enduring symbols, the Liberty Tree. Before the American Revolution, local chapters of the Sons of Liberty met beneath such trees in the 13 colonies. Hence, the Liberty Trees became symbols of America's War for Independence.

The 400-year-old tulip poplar was heavily decayed, but the damage inflicted by Hurricane Floyd proved irreversible. Arborist Russell Carlson, wrote, "Campers and wanderers, children and philosophers, vagrants and presidents have all stood in the shade of this ancient giant. But finally it is time to say goodbye."

A bell tolled 13 times for each of the original colonies. Crews went to work with chain saws. The wood was used for mementos and cuttings were taken for seedlings.

Think about the symbols that you value.

There is hope for a tree, if it is cut down, that it will sprout again, and that its shoots will not cease. (Job 14:7)

Jesus, remind us that there is no more potent symbol of Your love than Your cross.

Rebuilding a Life

Day after day, Vincent Jones, a fabric company worker, would pass Raymond Lawrence. Jones saw Lawrence, a homeless man who had become a fixture in Manhattan's Garment District, while making handcart deliveries. Then, for some reason he cannot explain, Jones determined to save Lawrence's life.

"I felt Raymond right here," Jones says, indicating his heart. "I truly saw God in that man's eyes when he told me he was hungry. I had never seen that before."

Lawrence had a mother living in Virginia who had given her son up for dead. Moreover, Lawrence was once a piano player. And so, after Lawrence had gone through an alcohol detox program, Jones drove him to his mother's home.

Today, Raymond Jones is the assistant music director at a church in Newport News and it's all thanks to a man who reached out to a stranger in need.

Someone needs you. You can change a life.

**Seek to do good to one another.
(1 Thessalonians 5:15)**

May I examine my heart and reach out, Lord Jesus.

Sister Scores

Sister Rose Ann Fleming seems to have the wrong job.

After eight years as president of Trinity College in Washington, D.C., eight as superintendent of Summit Country Day School in Cincinnati, Ohio, and 13 years teaching high school Latin and English, just what is she doing as academic adviser to 232 student-athletes at Cincinnati's Xavier University?

Sister Rose Ann not only loves the task she's been doing for 15 years, she also gets results. Since she started counseling, more than 90 percent of the school's student-athletes have graduated including 100 per cent of the men's basketball players.

"I honestly feel that helping a group of people understand the enhancement that education brings to their lives is important," she says. "It's very satisfying to me."

Helping others is satisfying. Satisfy yourself today.

Encourage the faint hearted, help the weak, be patient. (1 Thessalonians 5:14)

Father, You alone are my strength and consolation.

Violin Maker Inspires Life Lessons

John Sipe of Charlotte, North Carolina, is considered one of the finest violin makers in the country. While he doesn't teach his craft, there are lessons to be learned by watching him.

1: Find and commit to your calling. Inspired by the Golden Age of Italian violin making, from the late 16th to early 17th century, he quit his job as a furniture maker and began his lifelong pursuit.

2: Work for a great purpose. He believes the Lord wants him to craft wondrous violins. He prays for each person who plays one of his violins.

3: Be patient. Quality is everything: "If you're trying to make a violin in a hurry, you're defeated right away."

4: Let others praise you. Sipe says, "a man knows when he's done things well. You'll get your due."

It is truly a blessing when our work can help us get better, help us care, and teach us patience and love.

Find enjoyment in all the toil with which one toils. (Ecclesiastes 5:18)

Like violins, each of us is a work of Your art, Creator.

Her True Calling

Actor Jamie Lee Curtis became a best-selling children's book author because she can look at the world from a child's point of view.

Curtis wrote her first book in 1992, when her adopted daughter Annie turned five. Annie played a key role in her mother's second book, *Tell Me Again About the Night I Was Born*. Then *Today I Feel Silly & Other Moods That Make My Day* made the bestseller lists. She finds that writing builds her self-esteem.

Today, her attention is on her family and on writing. "You have to focus on what you want to be good at," Curtis points out. The once driven movie star has learned to slow down and let go, a life lesson she credits to her children. "My kids have taught me that the more and more I let go, the better. Let someone else try to rule the world. I don't want to."

Think about what's important to you.

Jesus said...have you never read, "Out of the mouths of infants and nursing babies you have prepared praise for yourself?" (Matthew 21:16)

Gracious God, help us be childlike, not childish.

Closer to God: Centering Prayer

Centering Prayer is a way to quiet down and be with God. In this form of prayer, "we put aside all thoughts, feelings, desires, imaginings that stand in our way of being totally with God," according to writer Robert O'Rourke.

In his exploration of Centering Prayer, O'Rourke has used the ideas and writings of Rev. Thomas Keating and Rev. Basil Pennington. He suggests these steps:

- Take a few minutes to relax. Become aware of God dwelling at the center of your being.
- Choose a single word that expresses to you God's fullness.
- Say the word over and over to help you refocus when you become distracted.
- After 15 to 20 minutes, pray the "Our Father" and return to your usual activities.

However you pray, pray with a grateful heart.

Be still, and know that I am God! (Psalm 46:10)

Abba, may I truly understand the message of the Psalms: 'Be still and know that I am God'.

Slay Those Dragons!

If you have children, you probably already know that J. K. Rowling is the best-selling author of the wildly popular Harry Potter series of fantasy novels.

She has endowed her wizard-hero with many qualities including bravery. "I admire it above almost every other characteristic," she says. "Bravery is a very glamourous virtue. That's why I love him so much. He's a fighter."

While many might consider Harry courageous because of his willingness to stick his neck out, even in life-threatening adventures, the author describes this aspect of his character in much more down-to-earth terms. She says he is brave when he stands up for himself against his aunt and uncle. They consistently do everything possible to make his life miserable.

Are you answering the call to bravery in your own life? Resolve not to let dragons, bullies or tough situations determine your state of mind.

Take courage. (Haggai 2:4)

Holy Spirit, source of all courage, grant me Your grace.

An Uphill Race

She may already have had her fifteen minutes of fame, but Debbie Armstrong isn't ready to walk or ski away quite yet.

During the 1984 Winter Olympics in Sarajevo, Armstrong took home the gold in the women's giant slalom. She was the first American to do so since 1952. In an interview with Sports Illustrated, she shared her memory of the "rainbow of color" she witnessed during the opening ceremonies, when Serbs, Muslims and Croats danced in unison.

Today, Armstrong has maintained her connection to the city which was devastated by more than three years of ethnic warfare. She serves as spokesperson for Global ReLeaf Sarajevo, which is committed to raising the funds necessary to plant 300,000 trees in the city and its environs.

"It may sound corny," she acknowledges, "but to give something back is very special."

Is there some debt of gratitude you can repay?

Be thankful. (Colossians 3:15)

Lengthen and strengthen our memories, Lord. Help us show generosity and gratitude to those who bless our lives.

Point...Click...Volunteer

All of us have heard of e-commerce, but what about e-volunteering? Jay Backstrand, president of Impact Online, a non-profit service that matches would-be volunteers with opportunities over the Internet, has helped pioneer this concept.

"Why shouldn't I be able to volunteer someplace the same day if I have a couple of hours," said Backstrand. Through his VolunteerMatch service people all over the United States can find and contact appealing service opportunities with the click of a mouse. So far about 75,000 volunteers have been matched with activities ranging from helping the homeless to planting trees.

And more lies ahead. Mr. Backstrand imagines volunteer groups using the data gleaned from the matching service in direct mail campaigns and large companies coordinating service activities for their employees through special volunteer sites.

Thanks to the vision and effort of one person, the lives of many will be touched. Make a difference in your own way.

Where are your righteous deeds? (Tobit 2:14)

Allow me to recognize my profound capacity to help those in need, God of Mercy.

Early Environmental Activists

In the 21st Century many people pride themselves on being environmentally sensitive.

Few today would question the importance of protecting Florida's Everglades. Nevertheless, there was a time when the precious wetlands were unappreciated. That changed because of the efforts of Marjory Stoneman Douglas.

"There would most likely be no Everglades wilderness without her," according to writer Stephen W. Byers.

Douglas was a Wellesley College graduate, a suffragist, a civil rights proponent and a newspaper editor as well as an environmentalist and writer. A South Florida resident, Ms. Douglas' 1947 book *The Everglades: River of Grass* forever changed the way people looked at the fragile environment. She called it "one thick enormous curving river of grass." She continued to work on behalf of the Everglades until her death in 1998.

What in your life is worth that much commitment? What are you doing about it?

The only thing that counts is faith working through love. (Galatians 5:6)

Guide us to appreciate nature's wonders, Creator.

Conversation Starters

Looking for meaningful conversations with your youngsters? *201 Questions to Ask Your Kids/Parents* by Pepper Schwartz offers ideas:

Questions for Parents:

What three adjectives would you use to describe me to a friend?

What are your favorite movies? Why?

What was the best present I ever gave you?

Who was your best friend in high school? Why?

What gift did you want as a kid and never got?

Questions for Kids:

If you could, with whom would you trade lives?

What is the most enjoyable thing our family has done in the past three years?

What is the most precious thing you own?

Name your three favorite movies.

What do I do that embarrasses you?

No relationship, no family, no organization can be strong and healthy without communication. Talk and listen.

(Jesus) spent the night in prayer to God. (Luke 6:12)

Support us in learning to talk to each other with love, Lord.

Seeing Music in the Darkness

After contracting diphtheria at age three, Joaquin Rodrigo went blind. Later, he came to believe that it was his blindness that led him to music by giving him a "greater inner world."

Rodrigo wrote his compositions in Braille, then dictated them, note by note, to a copyist. His large body of music was written for a variety of media and ages. In fact, some of his compositions were written just for children – not surprising for this devoted family man. This Spanish composer won a great number of prizes and honors for his work. And while he was a pianist, he also wrote music for the guitar.

Born on November 22, the feast day of St. Cecilia, patron saint of musicians, Rodrigo died in 1999 at age 97, maintaining to the end that his blindness had given him the greatest vision.

Open yourself to all God's wonders.

The eyes of the blind shall be opened. (Isaiah 35:5)

Help me to see others as You do, Father. Help me to love as You do.

Answering God's Call Despite Obstacles

Being illiterate, especially in modern society, is a mighty obstacle. But once Thomas Forbes heard a call to ordained ministry he wasn't about to let the shame of his long-held secret stop him from responding to God.

According to Forbes, it was 1969 when he heard "a call from God telling me to become more involved in the Church." That's the message he took from two heart attacks and forced retirement from his building trades work.

Thomas Forbes' illiteracy had kept him from a promotion to foreman. But he wasn't going to let it prevent him from studying for the deaconate. A quick learner, he studied with a tutor for a year and became an avid reader. He then enrolled in classes for the ministry and sweated when he first had to read aloud.

But eventually he was ordained a Deacon. About his life of service and prayer, Deacon Forbes says: "I have a beautiful life."

What does God ask of You?

We toil and struggle because we have our hope set on the living God. (1 Timothy 4:10)

God, help us to know and live Your will.

Food for Thought

Have you ever wondered how we got from the Earl of Sandwich in 1762 to fast food today? Or what it says about American ingenuity? *Newsweek* columnist George Will has.

There were times when the Earl of Sandwich partied day and night and was not inclined to stop for a sit-down meal. His solution?: "Eating meats placed between slices of bread." Fast forward to 1893 when the hot dog bun was born in Chicago. Sausage-seller Anton Ludwig Feuchtwager needed a practical way to keep customers from burning their fingers on his snacks.

With the 20th Century and the birth of the automobile industry, American drivers were on the move. Could Stuckey's or Steak 'N Shake be far behind? We don't even have to leave the car to buy and eat our meals.

Ingenuity. Where will it take us next? Whether you love fast food or think it's too, well, fast, the world is hungry for your good ideas.

**The clever do all things intelligently.
(Proverbs 13:16)**

Jesus, we celebrate the inventive spirit instilled within.

Just Leave a Note by the Phone

Now that their five children are on their own, Barbara and Gary Jayne have moved to a smaller house. Among the treasures Barbara unearthed as she packed were 19 spiral notebooks.

For seven years, the family left a notebook by the phone in the kitchen. Everyone learned to write in the book such pertinent information as where they were, who they were with, and when they would return.

They also included inspirational messages for each other. Although Barbara tried to keep her family on track with musings such as, "Let's all have a good Advent to prepare for Christ's birthday." A note to "Call the hospital" because Danny broke his arm is just as poignant. One of the last entries was a pool to guess the birth date of the first grandchild.

In this day of cell phones and voicemail, notebooks are a nice idea for those who want to recapture a simpler, richer time.

Remember the days of old, consider the years long past. (Deuteronomy 32:7)

In every activity, Lord, let us listen to each other and build each other up.

Thanks for Things We Complain About

Too often, in the rush and crush of busy lives, we forget to be thankful. What we so often whine and complain about are the same things we need to appreciate. According to writer Nancy Carmody, we should be thankful for:

- Taxes we pay because it means we're employed.
- Lawns that need mowing and windows that need cleaning because it means we have a home.
- A bill for winter oil or gas because it means we're warm.
- Complaints about government because we have freedom of speech.
- Clothes that are a little too snug because we have enough to eat.
- The alarm that goes off too early because it means that we're alive.

Try to offset the negativity that can weigh you down. At the end of a so-called bad day consider the blessings you enjoy.

Offer to God a sacrifice of thanksgiving. (Psalm 50:14)

I am thankful for all that I have, Generous Giver.

The Return of the Turkey

Had Ben Franklin gotten his way, the wild turkey, not the bald eagle, would have been selected to symbolize America.

Franklin believed wild turkeys were the ideal patriotic symbols. Adaptable, sociable and smart, the male even has red, white and blue plumage.

Sadly, by the middle of the 20th century, this grand bird was dangerously close to extinction. But thanks to an aggressive conservation program, the wild turkey is once again thriving in numbers, inhabiting every state but Alaska.

Wildlife and the environment are all part of not only Nature's delicate balance, but also our national history. Support efforts to conserve God's precious creations.

Are not five sparrows sold for two pennies? Yet not one...is forgotten in God's sight. But even the hairs of your head are all counted. Do not be afraid; you are of more value than many sparrows. (Luke 12:6-7)

Father God, thank You for all the wondrous beauty of Your creation.

Thanksgiving – No Vegetables, No Forks

Vegetables may have been present at the first Thanksgiving, but experts who recreate the historic harvest celebration at Plimoth Plantation in Massachusetts each year, doubt it.

"The emphasis was on beer, bread and flesh, not on vegetables," says Kathleen Curtin, who has been working at the plantation for the past dozen years. "This menu is the best the Pilgrims could have had."

The meal, in fact, includes no pies or cakes because historians doubt that the Pilgrims would have had an oven when this feast took place. There is, however, lobster (too common to be a treat for the Pilgrims). Oh and there were no forks. Forks were rare in Europe before the 18th century. For those who like to finish a meal with a cup of fine brewed coffee, you will get your wish at the celebration's recreation although you wouldn't have had that treat at the first Thanksgiving in 1621. London's first coffeehouse opened in 1657.

Enjoy meals with family and friends whenever possible.

With gratitude in your hearts sing...to God. (Colossians 3:16)

Thank You for Your bounty, Creator. You fill us full of all good things.

Sounds of Silence Spur Ideas

Librarians in Englewood, Colorado, don't get upset when books are returned past their due date in the days between Thanksgiving and Christmas.

In fact, with the library's "Food for Fines" program, patrons can pay their overdue book fines with a can of non-perishable food for each overdue book. The food is then distributed to needy families. In one year, the program raised $700 worth of food.

Across the country, in Ipswich, Massachusetts, librarians recently invited townspeople to withdraw as many books as possible – and to keep them home for a month. The library was in the midst of renovation and the staff had to find a place to store the collection. The program was a great success, and Ipswich – at least for one month – was the best read town anywhere.

There are solutions to problems if only a little imagination is applied.

The Lord created human beings. ...tongue and eyes, ears and a mind for thinking He gave them. (Sirach 17:1,6)

Spirit of God, bring me inspiration and hope.

A Jolly Good Life

Archibald Stiles' family couldn't afford to buy him toys as a child. Perhaps that's why he collected toys and oversaw a menagerie including deer, peacocks, ducks, turkeys, cats, a raccoon, and a crow.

He and his wife, Emma, also ran a magical little store that attracted collectors and browsers from the world over.

According to Stiles' obituary in *The New York Times,* he introduced a new aspect to his business in the 1950's. "When one manufacturer of ice skates had suffered a fire and another a strike," the paper reported, "skates were hard to find. The Stileses bought as many used skates as they could find. They invited others to trade in skates that no longer fit, charging $1 per trade.

With his portly frame and full white beard, more than one person commented on Archibald's resemblance to a certain resident of the North Pole. Assuring a supply of ice skates for youngsters certainly helped that resemblance.

There are so many ways to do something good and useful.

A generous person will be enriched.
(Proverbs 11:25)

Fill my heart with generosity, Lord, that others may recognize our resemblance.

A McFriendly Samaritan

Cindy Popola of Portland, Maine pulled up to a local McDonald's for a quick meal. As she trudged through the knee-high snow in the parking lot, she yanked off her gloves and heard a metallic "clink," but did not think much about it.

Later that day, she realized that the "clink" she had heard was her engagement ring and wedding band hitting the ground. She rushed back to the parking lot only to spend fruitless hours melting snow with buckets of hot water. Finally, Cindy Popola gave up hope.

But not McDonald's worker Don Rich. He searched the next day alone because, "I'd hate to see somebody lose something so dear." Goodwill and persistence paid off. Rich found both rings and returned them to their ecstatic owner.

This story is not about two bands of gold, but a heart of gold. Good Samaritans still exist. Don't be afraid to be one.

'Love...God with all your heart, and with all your soul...and your neighbor as yourself'. (Luke 10:27)

Give us the heart of the good Samaritan, Jesus.

A Home Run Decision

When Bo Jackson announced his retirement from baseball in 1994, it wasn't because of the baseball strike or the deterioration of his athletic skills or a problem with his artificial hip.

Jackson says he decided to head for home – and not home plate – because of something his son Nicholas asked his mother Linda.

Then six years old, Nicholas wanted to know why his father was never home. When he didn't receive a satisfactory response, Nicholas asked his mother if his dad had another family somewhere else.

At that point, Jackson says his choice was clear. "If that isn't enough for any man to make up his mind, then he isn't a man," says Jackson, "and he isn't a father."

We all have big decisions to make for the welfare of our families. Our options and opportunities as well as our attitudes and circumstances vary greatly. But we owe it to our loved ones to do the very best we can.

Decide with equity. (Isaiah 11:4)

Each and every day, Father, guide me and my loved ones with Your wisdom and protect us with Your love.

Of Asparagus and Cabbages

Kids today are enjoying videos and tapes featuring Larry the Cucumber, Bob the Tomato, and an assortment of other fruits and vegetables in the spectacularly successful series, VeggieTales.

Song titles ranging from "The Hairbrush Song" to "I Can Be Your Friend" present positive, Christian values in an enormously inventive setting. Part of the appeal is that the lyrics and messages are hitting home with adults as well.

"I'm busy, busy, dreadfully busy, you've no idea what I have to do! Busy, busy, shockingly busy, much, much too busy for you," croons one character. It's enough to give a person pause.

Founded by computer animator Phil Vischer in 1993, Big Idea Productions is focused on nothing short of becoming a top family media brand. "The world is full of companies out to make a buck," says Vischer. "The world desperately needs a company that is out to make a difference."

What's motivating you to succeed?

Human success is in the hand of the Lord. (Sirach 10:5)

Abba, let me hear your call to growth, even if it's through a child's song.

A Dental Retreat

Dennis and Bev Bedard went on retreat. At least that's the way it felt. In reality, the couple's two weeks in Quezon City, the Philippines, were spent pulling and filling teeth. Dennis, a dentist, ably assisted by his wife, Bev, helped close to 300 patients.

"Our two weeks with the people in the Philippines was like a retreat for us," says Bev Bedard.

For the past five years, Dennis has made annual spring visits to Guatemala where he volunteers his skills as a dentist, doing basic fillings and tooth extractions. On this trip his wife joined him.

"There are so many people," says the dentist. "You can be there a year and you'd never finish the work." Tooth decay is particularly prevalent because of a diet rich in sugar and poor in fluoride. In speaking about their service, Dennis Bedard explains: "God's been good to us and this is our way of giving back."

Do you put your gratitude to God into action?

What shall I return to the Lord for all His bounty to me? (Psalm 116:12)

I rejoice in all You have given me, Father. I praise You for Your overwhelming love.

Managing Stress

Christmas, Hanukkah, Kwanzaa – name a holiday or holyday and you name a time of stress for at least some people. Can you manage this tension? Sure. Here are some suggestions:

- Spend time with family and friends and at holiday events or holyday worship. You will cherish this, not complicated cooking, exhausting housecleaning or frantic gift buying.

- Ignore the hype and the "shoulds." You'll be happier and feel less pressure.

- Spend only what you can really afford to spend on gifts, food and beverages, clothes.

- Do something for the less fortunate. You'll gain perspective on what is important – people.

- Make every day warm and loving for the special people in your life and for yourself, not just a few days in the year.

Be gentle on yourself and those around you.

Little children, let us love, not in word or speech, but in truth and action. (1 John 3:18)

Thank You, Creator, for my family and friends.

Santa's Knows What's Real

Yes, Virginia there is a Santa Claus. His name is Daniel Jacobs. In 1984, fed up with the commercialism of Christmas, the father of five felt he had been missing the point of the holiday.

He did something about it. Jacobs started small, helping three needy families he had met working for customer service at the local power company. His efforts grew. Today, Christmas Families, the organization he founded, has hundreds of volunteers and supplies gifts to close to two thousand needy families and foster children in the Kansas City area. They try to "custom fit" the gift to each person they help.

Jacobs' vision has grown, but he remains at the core as the inspiration and the drive for the group. "There's just something about Daniel and the project that...reminds us what's real about Christmas," said one longtime volunteer.

What's real to you this Christmas? Getting? Giving to those who already have much? Think of the little Child of Bethlehem before you answer.

She gave birth to her firstborn son and wrapped him in bands of cloth, and laid him in a manger. (Luke 2:7)

Infant Jesus, be present in our Christmas preparations.

Enduring Bonds

Jean Carnahan wasn't looking for a career in politics. In fact, she had spent her entire married life thinking of herself as simply the spouse of a politician.

Then she lost her husband Mel Carnahan and their son, Roger, in a plane crash while Mel was campaigning for the United States Senate. "Your whole world stops moving," Jean Carnahan said. "You just don't know where to pick up or how to move forward." She found out how to do that through prayer.

"I thought about it a lot and I prayed about it," she says of her decision to accept the seat to which her husband was posthumously elected. United States Senator Jean Carnahan believes that a cause can motivate a life. "I think having something to do, a reason to get up in the morning, a cause – that has helped me."

What cause or larger purpose motivates your life?

A capable wife who can find?...Give her a share in the fruit of her hands, and let her works praise her in the city gates. (Proverbs 31:10, 31)

Help me to make opportunities out of obstacles, Lord.

Prayers, Answers and Work

When Melanie Sulivan's daughter was born with Cystic Fibrosis (CF), her world changed forever. Dreams of camping trips and amusement parks suddenly became secondary to medication and coughing exercises.

Sulivan had prayed daily since her Catholic school days. Throughout her pregnancy, she had prayed for a healthy baby. Suddenly it seemed like God hadn't been listening.

She became very involved in the local CF chapter. She sponsored car washes, clothing drives and an annual garage sale. She was determined to fund research for a cure, even if God wasn't helping her.

"I know now," she said, "that He was helping me all along. He inspired my ideas and facilitated my efforts. The money we raise will help my daughter and every other child with CF. I pray now in thanks instead of asking for anything. All we need, He is giving us."

Thank God for all the ways He sustains you.

I can do all things through Him who strengthens me. (Philippians 4:13)

Direct me, Creator, to do Your work on earth.

Words, Glorious Words

Who decides what slang gets into the dictionary and what is thrown into the dustbin of linguistic history?

Joseph Pickett for one. Pickett is the executive editor of the American Heritage Dictionary, and a lexicographer who determines whether words like "multitask" and "shock jock" will be enshrined on its pages (they will). "Stalkerazzi," made popular after Princess Diana's death, will not.

10,000 new entries made their way into the dictionary's fourth edition that were not in the third. Living languages are constantly changing. That's certainly true of American English, and often the changes reflect preoccupations of the day. Today, words related to technology dominate, but tomorrow who knows?

Choose your words with care and with respect for your listeners as well as yourself.

He sent letters to...every province in its own script and to every people in its own language. (Esther 1:22)

Help the nations and peoples of the earth speak the language of peace, Prince of Peace.

Battling the Holiday "Gimmes"

If you're a parent of young children, you are probably familiar with those Christmas "gimmes," those endless lists of "have to have" presents.

How do you combat this greediness and turn children into givers and not just getters? Here are a few tips:

- Since giving is more than seasonal, the other 11 months of the year set the tone of the holidays.
- Guard against peer pressure on your children and on yourselves. Remember, do what's right for your kids, your family.
- Give creative gifts. They don't have to cost a lot of money.
- Plan activities that emphasize Jesus' birth.
- Nurture an attitude of gratitude. Talk to your children about how fortunate you are as a family, and why.
- Can it be said too often? Show good example.

Above all, teach your children to balance giving and receiving. The reward will be year-round.

The righteous are generous. (Psalm 37:21)

Remind us that it is in giving that we receive, Giver of every good.

Key of Kindness

Rachel Downs woke early each morning to drive her husband to the train station. One winter day, the couple managed to lock their keys in the car while they were at the station.

Two service station attendants, one lock-smith and two hours later, the keys remained locked inside the Downs' car – with the couple stuck in the cold. Then a man approached. Hearing their situation, he handed them his own car keys, telling them to visit their car dealer for an extra set of keys. When they were done, they should just leave his car parked in the lot. Then a train pulled into the station and the man hopped on board.

Rachel Downs and her husband got their extra set of keys, and returned the man's car to the lot, leaving his keys and a note of thanks inside.

Make time in your day for kindness and gratitude.

The fruit of the Spirit is...patience, kindness, generosity. (Galatians 5:22)

This day, Father, help me to bring Your light and love to a world so in need of both.

The Craftsman and the Nutcrackers

78-year-old Christian Steinbach, dressed in lederhosen and a bright yellow Bavarian folk jacket, spends three months each year on tour in the United States.

With his good-natured manner, Steinbach patiently signs the nutcrackers brought to him by loyal collectors who stand in long lines. He has his picture taken with them and tells stories about the colorful nutcrackers which his family has been crafting for five generations. Even after a store closes, he stays to sign the beautifully crafted nutcrackers that fans have left behind.

What motivates this master craftsman to push himself so relentlessly? "I do it for my workers," he says, referring to his 320 German employees. "They trust me to bring back orders."

We depend on each other in so many ways. Poet-priest John Donne wrote "no man is an island entire of himself; every man is a piece of the Continent, a part of the main...I am involved in Mankind."

How does your work affect others?

Bear one another's burdens. (Galatians 6:2)

Fill us with energy and enthusiasm, Lord, as in concert with others we go about our work.

Peacemaker–With a Black Belt?

Don't let Darla Bolon's black belt in the martial arts fool you. She is committed to "increasing the peace" all around her.

As the coordinator of violence prevention and recovery services at Grant/Riverside Hospitals in Columbus, Ohio, Bolon has spent more than 18 years helping women reclaim their peace after rape or domestic violence. "I try to guide them toward finding power within (themselves)," she says. "My passion is teaching women skills that lessen their vulnerability to violence."

For example, to balance emotionally draining counseling sessions, Bolon offers self-defense and meditation classes to reduce symptoms of stress and bring more inner peace.

She adds, "My own proudest moments include getting my black belt. I want to help other women tap into their strengths and potential."

Find your strength and your peace in the Lord.

May you be made strong with all the strength that comes from His glorious power. (Colossians 1:11)

Jesus, be my ultimate source of strength.

The Person-Friendly Office

Many of us spend a large percentage of our waking hours at the office. Sometimes we forget that the people we work with are more than co-workers, and that everyone needs some degree of social interaction on the job. Here are several ideas for respecting each other and creating a friendly atmosphere in the office.

- Congratulate co-workers for important events like getting engaged or buying a house.
- When you enter a co-worker's office or call on the phone, always ask whether or not it's a convenient time.
- Be considerate when you make phone calls. Keep your voice down.
- If you see a fax with a co-worker's name, deliver it.

Being friendly and professional are not mutually exclusive. We are each unique and much loved children of God.

Be hospitable to one another. (1 Peter 4:9)

Loving God, give me insight into my co-workers, and help me to remember they, too, are Your beloved children.

Season of Giving and Receiving

As the single mother of five children, Joan was working three jobs just to pay the bills. She knew there wasn't enough money for holiday gifts.

Barbara understood. She had once been on welfare. At that time, she had prayed, "Will I ever have the opportunity to give to others?" Now, hearing about Joan's troubles, Barbara felt God saying, "Joan needs your assistance."

Barbara asked Joan what her children wanted for Christmas. She said, "this is your season for receiving." Thanks to a single parent leadership team that she had just formed at her office, Barbara soon had gifts for Joan's children – a train set, curling irons, toiletries.

Joan's thank-you letter later said they had turned one of her bleakest Christmases into an unforgettable one.

If you're feeling overwhelmed this holiday season, share your burden with someone; ask for help. Remember, God puts people in our lives to reach out to us.

Brother Saul the Lord Jesus...has sent me so that you may regain your sight and be filled with the Holy Spirit. (Acts 9:17)

Even in anxiety, Lord, help me know Your loving concern.

Give Yourself Christmas Gifts

Is the Christmas season leaving you feeling empty? Do most gifts seem to be a whole lot of glitter without substance? Try these four gifts this year:

The Gift of Financial Freedom. Plan your purchases; limit credit-card expenditures; give gifts of lasting value.

The Gift of Emotional Balance. Keep some traditions; change others; create special ones; remember the forgotten.

The Gift of Physical Care. Be weight conscious without being obsessive; exercise; get enough sleep.

The Gift of Spiritual Joy. Take time to be alone; remember the spirituality of the season; attend religious events; keep your spiritual life simple, focused.

This Christmas, treat yourself to these gifts and you'll be surprised at how full and fulfilling your holiday season will be.

If you...know how to give good gifts to your children, how much more will your Father...give good things to those who ask Him! (Matthew 7:11)

May I know the true joy of Your season, Christ Savior.

Mary's Place

In 1991, Mary Gonzalez lost her job when her department was eliminated. After dealing with the shock, she turned to God, asking for guidance.

Walking through her Chicago neighborhood, Gonzalez noticed families sleeping in their cars; hungry neighbors rooting through garbage cans for food. She decided she would help the poor in her community.

Now as many as 30 young people come to her home before and after school each day. They enjoy healthy recreation and snacks together, and know Gonzalez is always willing to listen.

"These kids need a feeling that somebody loves them and will be there for them," she asserts.

Ashlet Holimon agrees. "This keeps me out of street trouble," she says. "If I wasn't here, I'd probably be in the back of a police car."

How can you welcome poor people into your life?

As you did it to one of the least of these who are members of My family, you did it to Me. (Matthew 25:40)

Let me not be afraid to get involved and get to work in service to my brothers and sisters, God.

Always the Perfect Fit

Want to give a gift this Christmas that doesn't cost anything and that will be the perfect gift for the person receiving it? You can.

Give a personal gift coupon – a pledge of service or a promise of fun. Such gift coupons also extend Christmas gift-giving long after the tree has been taken down and the ornaments stored away.

A coupon for parents could be a promise to help around the house or the garden. A coupon for a grandparent could offer a "Saturday together, however you want to spend it." With siblings close in age, coupons good for taking over the other's household chores for a limited time is appropriate and surely welcome.

Personal gift coupons are gifts of your attention, your interest, your time, your self. And they can be a reminder of the one whose birth Christmas celebrates, Jesus, who gave His time, His service, His very self for each one of us.

The Son of Man came not to be served but to serve, and to give His life a ransom for many. (Mark 10:45)

We thank You, Lord, for the gifts You have given us.

Patience, Vision and a Walk in the Park

Patience is a virtue; but what does it really mean? For Frederick Law Olmsted it meant the difference between a sloppy, ill-conceived creation and something that would grow in elegance and beauty long after its creator was gone.

Olmsted is best known for designing New York's Central Park. A landscape architect before there was such a title, Olmsted was a nineteenth century Renaissance man who won the commission for the design of the park on the strength of his tour of European gardens, an intense practicality and a sweeping vision of what a public space in a growing metropolis should be.

Central Park's ponds, meadows and vistas are a testament to Olmsted's vision and also to his supreme patience. "We determined," Olmsted told his son Rick about his plan for the park, "to think of no results to be realized in less than forty years."

What do you plan to leave behind for the next generation?

The plans of the diligent lead surely to abundance, but everyone who is hasty comes only to want. (Proverbs 21:5)

Holy Spirit, give us the wisdom to make plans; the patience to work and wait for their fulfillment.

Simplifying Christmas

If your goal is to make the holidays more meaningful, evaluate your family traditions. Which are your favorites? Which most meaningful? Which need to be dropped?

Once you clear out the clutter, consider some of the following ideas:

- Go caroling with family and friends. End the evening with hot chocolate and cookies, and a reading of the Nativity story.
- Let your children bake a birthday cake for Jesus. Share it with family, friends and neighbors.
- Make a Christmas scrapbook for your favorite snapshots of Christmases past and present.

However you celebrate in your home, be sure the traditions are really meaningful. Center your celebrations on the real reason for Christmas and you can't go wrong.

A Child has been born for us...and He is named Wonderful Counselor, Mighty God, Everlasting Father, Prince of Peace. (Isaiah 9:6)

Infant Jesus, help us prepare for Your birthday.

Little Dolls Serve Large Purpose

Gretchen Wilson and Colleen Charleston are the co-founders of Little Souls Inc., a company that makes popular dolls.

Since they began the company in 1986, their distinctive dolls have appeared on TV and have become collectibles. Though thrilled by their success, the two feel Little Souls serves a larger purpose.

The production crew includes ex-welfare mothers, a former homeless person and immigrants from Nigeria and Cambodia. Charleston and Wilson provide daycare programs.

The dolls' clothing is made by poor women in places like Tibet and Ghana. "They're generating a higher quality of life for people in developing nations," says Christopher Gallagher, president of a group of philanthropic entrepreneurs.

Wilson and Charleston never lose sight of their commitment to doing good. Charleston says that if it all ended tomorrow, "we can look at each other and say that was a job well done – and aren't we blessed?"

Take time out today to count your blessings.

Continue to live your lives in Him...abounding in thanksgiving. (Colossian 2:6,7)

Holy One, may my blessings benefit others.

O Christmas Tree

A $5 tip that was refused, brought a little Christmas joy into the life of columnist Rick Shefchik.

He and his family purchased their Christmas tree at a nursery. A teenager hauled the tree out to their car. Then, taking off his gloves, he wrapped the tree in twine and scooted under the snow-covered car to secure it to the bumper.

"There's little holiday charm in doing these tasks in sub-zero weather," Shefchik noted. He offered the boy a $5 tip. The young man refused it, saying it was merely his job.

Driving away from the lot, Shefchik reflected that "I met a nice kid who worked hard on a cold day and didn't want anything extra for it," he said. "I hope he has a wonderful Christmas."

Generosity usually means giving, but it could mean not accepting a gift. Whatever you do, be open-hearted in all things.

The measure you give will be the measure you get, and still more will be given you. (Mark 4:24)

Help us remember, Lord, that generosity leads to generosity.

The Best Medicine and More

"Every night after dinner, I play bridge with the youngsters down the hall," says Margaret Craft. Those "youngsters" are in their seventies and eighties; Ms. Craft, a feisty 102.

There are more than 50,000 centenarians in America today, and their ranks are increasing. Some estimate that by the year 2050, the number will rise to three million. The good news is that many of those living long lives are living them in good health.

While doctors still consider those who reach the 100-year-mark to be in "extreme old age," and while genes certainly play a role, four centenarians interviewed by *Family Circle* magazine had certain common characteristics. They eat a lot of vegetables; don't smoke; have hobbies and interests; and said that visiting friends and family or helping others was their greatest pleasure.

Dr. Margery Silver made one additional observation: centenarians laugh a lot. That's worth considering, at any age.

Teach us to count our days that we may gain a wise heart. (Psalm 90:12)

Only You know how many days I have on this earth, O Lord. Help me approach them with delight.

Same Customs, Different Worlds

It's sometimes surprising to see how people from different parts of the world can be so similar. Take Christmas holiday customs, for example. Juana Alvia says Christmas in her native Ecuador is very similar to Christmas in the United States, because "the focus is on the family being together," she says.

Issolina Varrosso, 65, reminisces about her childhood Christmases in Italy. Her family would roast chestnuts, light a fire in the fireplace, and stuff stockings with goodies for all.

Svetlana Vilbaum's story is different. In the Ukraine she says, "We couldn't celebrate any holidays, that's why we came here. We celebrate everything, and we're happy."

We have much in common with people who might seem far away both geographically and culturally than we might think at first. It seems that it's just human to want to celebrate.

Rejoice in the Lord! (Psalm 97:12)

Jesus, remind me to look for what unites people, rather than what divides them.

Peace and Good Will at Christmas

St. Paul Lutheran Church burned to a charred frame on Christmas Day, 1995. Pastor Richard Robinson thought an old building on the Dallas church's property could be restored as a temporary church and Sunday-school building. But the small African-American congregation did not have the means to repair it.

Judy Lipman Nassif decided to get her synagogue involved and asked them to declare St. Paul a "mitzvah." Donations accumulated and less than a month later the building had been rehabilitated. Workers and church members gathered for prayers. For some, it was their first significant contact with another religion.

Said Nassif, "With understanding comes acceptance." Touched by the kindness they were shown, St. Paul's parishioners have renewed their commitment to the needy in their community. Church secretary Barbara Fluker says, "Judy's generosity" made us realize that "even our little congregation can still help those in need."

God counts on us to love one another.

Do good to one another and to all.
(1 Thessalonians 5:15)

How can I spread Your message of good will to all, Lord?

Think Small

"Think small" seems to go against the grain for many of us. Yet it's possible that by doing so, you will make more of a difference than you realize. In his book, *Heaven on Earth*, Danny Seo outlines small ways in which you can have a positive impact on your world. Here are a few:

- donate your frequent flyer miles to a charity
- pass along your used golf clubs or other athletic equipment or donate the price of lessons so youngsters can learn
- see if your local animal shelter can use your old newspapers for bedding; or volunteer at an animal shelter
- donate time to your local PTA
- pass along used videos and CD's to your local library

We may be so used to thinking that only large gestures matter that we neglect little opportunities. You don't have to give a million dollars to a charity to be a philanthropist. Small gestures can be very big to someone else.

Be rich in good works, generous. (1 Timothy 6:18)

Help us, Lord, to appreciate small acts of kindness.

"Just" A Mom?

What's wrong with being "just" a mom? Nothing, according to Lynn Bowen Walker, a Stanford University graduate and a stay-at-home mother of two boys.

Walker is proud of doing what is right for her. She often encounters people who can't believe that she "gave up" a career and must sometimes "block out the covers of magazines that feature moms who seem to 'have it all'."

But Walker hears God say, "Stop looking at other people, I have something else in mind for you."

That something else is finding precious and irreplaceable gifts in what she calls "the peanut-butter-and-jelly moments." It is these moments that show her that her constant presence in her children's lives enables her to teach "them about love and faith and forgiveness."

People need to think through the big decisions of life, to pray and then choose what is right for them.

Those who respect their mother are like those who lay up treasure. (Sirach 3:5)

Inspire us to support all families, Father.

Get in the Game

Golf wunderkind Tiger Woods was named Sportsman of the Year by *Sports Illustrated* magazine at 24.

The issue included interviews with people who knew the golfer. The comments of Peter Kessler, host on the Golf Channel, were included.

Kessler remembered having met Tiger Woods at a golf club in Orlando. "We started talking very casually," Kessler remembered. "It wasn't the Tiger you see at his press conferences. It was the real Tiger." What impressed Kessler was the young golfer's love for the pressure of the game, win or lose.

"(Tiger) talked about winning easily at Bay Hill and losing that battle with Hal Sutton at the Players Championship," Kessler reported. "I was left with the strong impression that he enjoyed the Players far more."

Success can be wonderful, but if that's all that matters, we will lose out on a great deal of what makes life worthwhile.

Take nothing for your journey. (Luke 9:3)

Keep me tuned into the lessons of the journey, Savior, and less focused on always coming out on top.

Volunteering a Hand

Do you admire people who volunteer to help others, maybe even promise yourself that when you have more time you'll volunteer too?

Face it, that day will never come. Work, chores, family and social obligations eat up most waking hours. Don't lose heart. It's never been easier to turn your good intentions into action.

If you can only spare a day here or there, City Care has affiliates across the country. For example, Boston Cares' monthly newsletter lists more than 60 one-time or short-term opportunities.

If you decide to volunteer regularly, consider teaching someone to read. The Literacy Volunteers of America have chapters in 43 states. Build a house through Habitat for Humanity. Or help at a local homeless shelter or mission. Ask about volunteer activities at your house of worship.

If you truly want to volunteer, something will fit into your schedule. The gratification you will feel is immeasurable.

As you did it to one of the least of these who are members of My family, you did it to Me. (Matthew 25:40)

I will not hesitate to reach out to others, Lord of Light.

No Matter Your Faith

Prayer on your behalf by others without your awareness helps.

In 1999, the Duke Clinical Research Institute in North Carolina conducted a study that proved this. In addition to formal care, half of a group of 150 patients with recurrent chest pain or serious heart attacks were prayed for – without their knowledge – by Carmelite nuns, Buddhist monks and the members of a Unity Church congregation in Maryland. The prayed-for group had "adverse outcomes" reduced 50 to 100 percent relative to the standard therapy group.

Studies of intercessory prayer raise many intriguing ethical and practical questions. But as one researcher said, "Is prayer associated with (relieving) illness? Yes. And that's why we're interested in prayer studies."

Don't wait for adversity before you pray. The strength and peace of true faith can enrich our lives every day.

Lord, teach us to pray. (Luke 11:1)

Keep me constantly aware of Your protection, Divine Master.

Time After Time

Columnist Ellen Goodman takes an unconventional approach to New Year's resolutions.

"The whole idea is to get a clean slate and a fresh start," she observes. Why, then, she asks, is the first assignment of the year to pick up our autobiography and begin to correct it?

Surveying popular lists of resolutions ranging from dieting to tightening budgets, Goodman wonders what would happen if our commitments weren't about narrowing life but widening it. "What about resolving to begin or enjoy rather than stop and repent?" she asks.

Goodman proposes developing two lists: This is What Matters to Me and, This is How I Spend my Time. "In the middle," she writes, "our resolution: to make the right side align with the left." She sums up the outcome she seeks in just five words: "To make our time matter."

Resolve to make your time matter.

A thousand years in Your sight are like yesterday...or like a watch in the night. (Psalm 90:4)

What is it, Creator God, that You would next like to teach me about Yourself? About myself? About Your universe?

Also Available

If you have enjoyed this volume of *Three Minutes a Day,* these other Christopher offerings may interest you.

- **News Notes** – published ten times a year on a variety of topics. Single copies, as published, are free; bulk and standing orders are welcomed.

- **Ecos Cristóforos** – Spanish translations of selected News Notes are issued six times a year. Individual copies are free; bulk and standing orders can be placed.

- **Appointment Calendars and Monthly Planners** – offer inspirational messages and scripture verses as well as practical formats.

- **Videocassettes** – Christopher videocassettes range from children's specials to one-on-one interviews on personal, social and spiritual issues.

For more information on The Christophers or to receive **News Notes, Ecos Cristóforos** or catalogs:

The Christophers
12 East 48th Street, New York, NY 10017
Phone: 212-759-4050
Web site: www.christophers.org
E-mail: mail@christophers.org

The Christophers is a non-profit media organization founded in 1945. We share the message of personal responsibility and service to God and humanity with people of all faiths and no particular faith. Gifts are welcome and tax-deductible. Our legal title for wills is The Christophers, Inc.